ASK AND KNOW

QUESTIONS FOR FIRMS AND SELF

ANSHUMAN SHARMA

To all those organizations and people who want to discover and transform.

Contents

Contents

Preface

Our organizations, in which we work or we own, are our workplaces and we spent most of our productive time there. But, even after committing a big part of our life to our companies, institutions, associations, corporations, and organizations, we know a little about these places. Few people in most organizations can understand the purpose of their entity or the objective of their work. In the case of understanding the values, and culture or defining the customers of the organization the number is even less. These people feel less connected or even disconnected from the organizations.

The same is true for a large percentage of humanity, which does not know the objective of their life or work. Many people feel that their destinies are being controlled by other people, and they can do nothing about it. People complain about their life, without knowing what they want, from life or work. They have difficulty getting clarity in any area of their life.

In this book, we will try to bring that clarity into the minds of the managers of the organizations, and normal people, to get hold of their lives. We will use the model based on the fundamental five questions for NGOs and nonprofit organizations. These questions are holistic and touch upon every area of the organization and a person's life. Answering these questions is not simple, even though the questions look easy. They dig deep into the foundations of our basic assumptions and present actions. You need to be ready to answer a lot of questions in this book. But after completing this book, and when many questions are answered, you would start to see things differently, and would get more control over your life, and your actions.

Prologue

Who would need this book?

The following readers can get the maximum benefit from the ideas presented in this book.

- Anyone who wants to review their organization from the fundamental perspective, to identify the weak areas, and strengthen the organization's position in the market.
- Individuals who want to bring clarity in their lives with a guided thinking process.
- Learners who want to enhance their knowledge through fundamental questions.
- People who want to exercise their minds with serious rounds of questions.

What can you expect after completing this book

- Getting **clarity about the present status of your organization,** in terms of its fundamentals, and the **ways to improve or transform it.**
- Your skills in answering the general questions will enhance appreciatively, as you will be answering a lot of questions in this book.
- You will **understand yourself better** and would know the **path to your success.**
- The deep introspection process during the book would **open your mind** to look at the hidden, misunderstood, and false areas of your organization and your life.

What is expected from the learners

- The learners have the freedom to take the book as they want, but it would be beneficial that they follow the flow of the book. Once the book is complete, they can choose any topic to reinforce the concepts by listening to specific lectures again.

- It would be important to complete the book, as all the topics and ideas are synergistically connected to each other.
- We expect learners to do all the exercises and follow the instructions as specified in each lecture, which would allow them to strengthen their concepts.
- This book is to build the fundamentals of self-analysis. The learners should not stop there, instead, they should look for resources and books to enhance their knowledge about self-analysis and to dig deeper to get more understanding about their organization and self.

Qualifications required to get the maximum benefit from the book

- There is no minimum qualification for this book, anyone who wants to understand the fundamentals of their organization and introspect about themselves can use this book.
- You need to be committed enough to complete the book and do its exercises with complete sincerity.

How to do it

- To get the maximum value out of this book, you need to start from the beginning and move step by step forward. Follow the book with its flow. This is important, as to understand a topic, we need to get clarity about its previous topics.
- It is required that you follow the instructions as specified in each section. Following the instructions would help you to become a better learner in the book.
- It is suggested that even if we have some brief understanding of a specific portion, it would be beneficial that we complete those topics in the book. It would act like a good revision for the subject, and act as an opportunity

to build momentum for completing the book.
- After understanding a specific portion of the book, you need to utilize the momentum to learn the topic from other resources and books.

What is in it for the learners

- Learn about asking the most fundamental questions for your NGOs and Non-profit organization.
- Analyze your for-profit organization by answering the specified questions.
- The answers to these questions would help you to set the right goals, both long-term and short-term.
- It is a tool for self-introspection.
- It would help you with innovation
- It will allow you to review your risks again, and identify fresh ways to manage them.
- It would question each and every assumption and perception used to develop a mission, strategy, and plan.
- It can be an opportunity to transform yourself and your organization

The Five Questions

The Five Questions

Now let us discuss the questions, which are required for an organization's introspection. These questions must be asked by the leaders and managers and must be understood by its employees and workers and other stakeholders, to serve their customers, markets and community better.

These questions look simple, but they have depth. Before answering these questions, it is necessary to understand their real meaning. It is necessary, as without understanding the questions, it would be difficult to answer them effectively.

CHAPTER TWO

The Five Questions

The Five Questions

In the simplest form, the questions can be specified in a few words, questioning the fundamentals of the business.

1. What is our mission?
2. Who is our customer?
3. What does the Customer Value?
4. What are our results?
5. What is our plan?

We will go into the depth of each of these questions in the coming sections of the book.

Questions Introduction

Every business has overflowing ideas, opinions, and suggestions of all types, good and bad. Some of these ideas point in completely different directions. Instead of giving clarity, these arrays of popping ideas confuse the managers, making the task of taking decisions, complex. They have difficulty identifying their direction and focus. It is important to know the goal, on which the organization's resources and efforts would be directed.

Answering these five questions would provide managers with complete clarity and help them to take decisions. These five questions have helped hundreds of organizations and thousands of managers in taking better decisions and directing their resources for success.

If managers seriously take these questions and answer them, then they would be able to reveal several elements, which were hidden from plain sight. Answering these questions should not be taken casually, instead, they should be a focused effort of the team of managers, leaders, and employees.

These questions may look easy, but as we introspect, we can see the depth hidden in each of these questions. They are not simple to answer, instead, they will touch upon almost all the important aspects of the organization and strategy. In many cases, the answers to these questions have questioned the strategy followed by the managers of the company. It has even compelled them to change it. These questions focus on fundamentals and challenge the status quo.

Why these questions

The objective of these questions

- To allow the managers to take stock of their present situations and conditions.
- To force them to introspect about the business.
- To make the managers ponder on the fundamental aspects of their business
- To bring necessary and required changes to the organization.
- Orienting the organization to bring in the synchronization with customers' needs and their satisfaction.
- For enhancing the strength and growth of the organization.

Question 1– What is our mission?

Let's now start with the fundamental questions. The first question is "what is our mission?"

Question 1- What is our mission?

Our Mission?

Let's now start with the fundamental questions. The first question is "what is our mission?" This is the fundamental question that questions the basic purpose of the existence of the corporation. Every organization exists with a specific mission, which could be explicit or implicit, which means that either it is clearly specified in words or implicitly understood by the managers of the organization. For example, most of the small-scale sector organizations, do not have a very clearly defined mission, but the shareholders and the managers of the organization know clearly about their business, and the actions they are going to take for the growth of their companies.

In the case of midsize to big companies, most of the companies have a clearly defined mission statement, which is displayed prominently in their offices and cabins. Whether they get some value out of it is a different question.

What Is Our Mission?

Q1- What is our mission?

We need to first understand the concept of the mission statement in the context of an organization.

A mission is a simple sentence describing a company's function, markets, and competitive advantages. It is a short written statement of the business goals, values, and philosophies it follows.

A mission statement defines:

1. **What an organization is**- It isthe definition of the organization, which brings a clear picture of its objectives, functions, and operations into the minds of the listeners and readers
2. **Why it exists**- The reason for the existence of the organization. These reasons could be the basic objectives for which the organization is existing, and serves its customers and society.
3. **Its reason for being**- What is the mission of the organization and how does it plan to achieve it? The mission of the organization is a long-term goal, which the organization wants to achieve. The managers and other stakeholders of the organization work towards achieving those goals by breaking them into medium-term and short-term goals.

A mission is a short statement of an organization's purpose, identifying the scope of its operations: what kind of product or service it provides, its primary customers or market, and its geographical region of operation. It may include a short statement of such fundamental matters, as the organization's values or philosophies, a business's main competitive advantages, or a desired future state— which can be called the "vision".

According to Chris Bart, who is a professor of strategy and governance at McMaster University, a commercial mission statement consists of three essential components:

1. **Key market**: Who is your target client or customer (*you can generalize if needed*)?
2. **Contribution**: What product or service do you provide to that customer?
3. **Distinction**: What makes your product or service unique, so that the potential customer would choose you?

Mr. Bart estimates that in practice, only about ten percent of mission statements say something meaningful. For this reason, they are widely regarded with contempt.

Every business has a specific purpose for its existence, which is to serve its customers, shareholders, and markets uniquely. This could be through a series of products or services. This purpose needs to be simple and understood clearly by everyone associated with the organization. The mission statement is generally specified in concise and clear words, which can easily be grasped by all stakeholders. (*Stakeholders are the people, institutions, and organizations, which are associated with the corporation in some way. These include customers, employees, shareholders, suppliers, and managers*). It is said that "the effective mission statement is short and sharply focused. It should fit in a T-shirt. The mission statement sees 'why you do, what you do'."

The mission is like a force, which is holding the corporation together. Employees get clarity about their daily tasks and goals, while customers and suppliers feel connected to the organization. Every planning process begins with the mission, as it always sits at the core. It is also important to understand, what is not to be changed. There are some fundamental and core values, which can never be changed for the organization. Based on the latest trends and the changes in the market, customer behavior, and technology, the mission statement can be reinterpreted with the help of new questions or can be slightly modified based on the present reality.

We need to keep asking:

What is our purpose?

The purpose of the organization is the basic objective for which it exists and functions. Till it is clear in the minds of the managers and other employees, they will not be able to work together for a common purpose and goal.

Why do we do what we do?

It is about understanding the "why?" to get daily guidance in our decisions and actions. The reasons for which our managers and employees work hard should be common and must be clearly understood by them. It is also important that other stakeholders of the organization are also clear about the "Why?" of the organization.

What do we want to be remembered for?

Every person, institution, association, and organization wants to leave a legacy, for which they want to be remembered. It is about the brand image, which the organization would leave in the minds of its customers and society. That is an important aspect of getting success in the marketplace. Organizations spend billions of dollars in building powerful brand images in the minds of the customers, which allows them to build trust and connect with the organization.

What is our mission in brief

Coming back to our first question, what is our mission? It is important that an organization understand the concept of mission and should define its mission clearly. It should then communicate it to all its stakeholders, which includes management, employees, customers, suppliers, and other partners. The mission statement would give clarity to everyone about the purpose of the organization and its existence. It will also help the managers by giving a clear direction to develop strategy and goals to pursue. It would also define the actions to be taken and the trade-offs to be made. Trade-offs means during a certain situation, when we have the option for several directions, then the mission statement gives us clarity about the direction and the decision to be taken.

CHAPTER FIVE

What is our mission – Sub-questions

Now let us dig deeper into fundamental question 1, which is, 'what is our mission?' In this section, we will cover a large number of sub-questions, which can help us to understand our mission and other concepts related to it.

The right way to do this section is to first understand the meaning of each question and answer it broadly in your mind. After each question, you should pause for some time to answer the question in your mind, without writing it down. Do it for each and every question. There could be some questions, which are not relevant to you, and can be skipped. It is up to you to identify the questions relevant to you and answer them sincerely. We can assure you that once the questioning of this section is over, you would know enough about your organization and its mission.

Once you have reached the end of the section, we suggest you come back and again start the questions from the beginning, and repeat the process. Capture your answers. You need to understand that only thinking about the answers in the mind is not enough, most of the time it is vague, and not clear. Once you write your ideas and understanding down on a piece of paper or digitally, then you have truly answered the question.

Just like this section, we will be having several other sections attached to each of the fundamental questions.

Let's move to questions.

What is our mission?

This first question constitutes a few sub-questions which are:
What is the current mission?

It means understanding the existing mission of the organization. Here we have to think about, What is our present understanding of the mission of our organization? Do other stakeholders of the organization understand it in a similar way? Is it explicitly written or is it implicit? How the difference in the understanding of the mission affects the functioning of the organization?

1. Why does our organization exist in the first place?

    - Specify the purpose of the existence of the organization.
    - Are we working honestly and effectively to achieve that purpose?
    - Are we satisfied with it? If not, why?
    - What do we need to do to bring our actions in synchronization with the true purpose of our organization?

2. What are we trying to accomplish for our customers?

    - Why our customers are associated with us?
    - What unique we are doing for them so that they remain loyal to us?
    - How hard we are trying to make our customers satisfied?

3. What values (principles) would lead us there?

    - Every organization has some unwritten rules which everybody follows. These are mostly implicit, not explicitly written somewhere. It would be great if we think about them in depth. What is the culture of our organization?
    - What principles or rules do we follow?
    - Does everyone in the organization agree with these principles? Do we follow them?
    - Many times we have certain rules which are designed after thinking to make our organization strong, but we rarely follow them. How our organization will change if they start following all the specified principles strictly?

4. Why do we have this mission?

- What are the reasons associated with the design of the present mission?
- Why do we have a specific mission for our organization?
- What is its origin?
- In what way this mission is adding value to us?
- Are our decisions and actions linked to this mission?

5. What do each word and their combination indicate, in the mission statement?

- Is the written meaning of the words in the mission statement and their implied meaning the same?
- What are the reasons for any difference?
- Is our mission able to answer the complex questions of the organization and help us in taking decisions?

6. What are the explicit and implicit meanings of that?

- Are the explicit and implicit meanings of the mission statement the same?
- How much implicit meaning is different from the explicit meaning in the mission statement?
- How are these differences affecting the functioning of the organization?
- How these meanings have changed over the period?
- What are the reasons for it?

7. Do we understand our mission?

- Does everyone in the organization understand the true meaning implied by our mission statement?
- How can we say that with surety?
- Has any test or analysis been done for it?

8. Do people in the organization interpret it in different ways?

- If there is any difference in interpretation, then what are the reasons for it?

- What actions have been taken to synchronize the mission understanding, that is to synchronize the intended meaning and the different interpretations?

9. What are the different perceptions of the mission by different stakeholders?

  - There can be several stakeholders in an organization. These are the people, groups, associations, or firms who are associated with our organization in some way. These could be our employees, customers, suppliers, partners, distributors, and many others. Different stakeholders can have different interpretations of our mission statement. How different stakeholders of the organization are interpreting the mission?
  - What actions do we need to take to synchronize the intended meaning of the mission and their understanding of the mission statement?

10. Do our present actions in synchronization with our mission?

  - Review your present actions, strategy, and planning and check if the mission of the organization dictates it. If not, we need to check for the discrepancy and find the reasons for it. If the mission and our actions are not in synchronization, then it would be difficult to focus the organization's efforts and resources.

11. Which are the actions and decisions, which do not meet our current mission?

  - We need to identify our actions and decisions, which are not in synchronization with our specified objective in mission. We need to identify the reasons for it. If there is any need for any changes or modifications then it must be done.

12. Do our all stakeholders understand our mission?

  - We need to make sure that all our stakeholders understand the mission of the organization and the direction we are taking. They also need to know the "why" for it, and the reasons we are following the specific mission. Till all our stakeholders are not connected with our mission, we will not be able to focus all our efforts and resources on common goals.

13. What are the reasons that stakeholders are not clear about the mission?

   ◦ All the managers and employees of the organization must know the importance of the mission and what should be the driving force for daily actions and decisions. If the stakeholders of the organizations are confused about the mission, then we need to find the reasons for it so that it could be corrected.

14. What can be the best way to communicate the mission to our stakeholders?

   ◦ The mission and any modification to the mission must be communicated to all the managers, employees, and other stakeholders of the organization. We need to identify the best ways to communicate the mission to them so that it is clear to them, and they feel connected to it. We can utilize the latest communication technology or social networking sites. It would be great if everybody involved have an open discussion to clear their doubts about it.

15. Does the mission dictate its goals and objectives?

   ◦ The objective of the mission is to give clear goals and objectives to all the managers and other employees of the organization. It is the responsibility of the senior management to make sure that the mission statement is converted to the individual goals of the employees and groups.

16. Are our strategy and plans in coordination with the mission? If not, what are the reasons?

   ◦ We need to regularly check and review our strategy and plans and check their synchronization with the mission of the organization. There could be instances when they are not in complete sync. We need to find the reasons for it and make the necessary corrections. Even if the strategy is not in synchronization with the mission of the organization, we need to take corrective measures.

CHAPTER SIX

What are our challenges?

What challenges our organization is facing?

We need to understand the challenges presently faced and to be faced by our organization, so that we could prepare for them. We need to look for creative ways to convert the challenges into opportunities.

1. What challenges we are facing- both internal and external?

    ◦ An organization faces different types of challenges both from inside the organization, which can be controlled, and from outside the organization, which can be managed. We need to understand both and take the required measures to either convert them into opportunities or manage them effectively.

2. How serious they are?

    ◦ We need to understand the seriousness of each of the challenges, both internal and external so that we can understand the priority level to deal with them.

3. How are they affecting us?

    ◦ It is important to understand the impact of the challenges on our organization. It would be required to develop strategies for the challenges.

4. How do these challenges affect our mission?

    ◦ Do these challenges have any effect on our mission?

- How can we make sure that any of the risk or challenge does not affect our driving force?

5. Is our mission providing the right guidelines and direction to meet these challenges?

   - Do we understand our mission statement enough to get the required directions for dealing with our challenges?
   - Is there any need to enhance our mission statement?

6. Are we able to take the required action to deal with the challenges?

   - What actions we are taking to deal with these challenges?
   - Are we satisfied with our actions and confident about their success?

7. Can we convert our challenges into our strengths?

   - Is there any way to convert some of our challenges into opportunities by enhancing our strengths?

8. How are our strengths and weaknesses affecting our challenges?

   - You need to know about the strengths and weaknesses of organizations and how they make you strong or vulnerable. We need to understand the relationship between our strengths and weaknesses with the challenges we face. How can the enhancement of our strengths affect our challenges?

9. What can we do to improve our position to deal with challenges?

   - Try to identify strategies and ideas to deal with your challenges effectively.

10. What resources we would need?

    - What are the resources, which would be required to exploit the challenges or to effectively deal with them?

11. How can we arrange for these resources?

    ◦ What is our plan to arrange for the identified resources?

12. How sensitive we are to these challenges (how hard they will affect us?)?

    ◦ What is our sensitivity analysis for these challenges? It is an analysis in which we know about the impact of the challenges on us.
    ◦ How can we strengthen our position against these challenges?

13. How do we analyze risk?

    ◦ What are our risks?

14. What is our risk management plan?

    ◦ What is our plan to manage our risks?

15. How is our risk in comparison to competitors?

    ◦ Are our risks more or less in comparison to our major competitors?
    ◦ What is our learning from this analysis?

16. Is the process standardized?

    ◦ Do we have a standardized process for analyzing risk and its management?

17. Can we improve our risk management?

    ◦ Think about the ideas to improve your risk management process and strategies.

CHAPTER SEVEN

What are our opportunities?

Just like our challenges we need to know about the opportunities which are available to us.

1. What are opportunities for us?

    ◦ Define the meaning of opportunity for yourself. What is an opportunity for you?
    ◦ What is not an opportunity for you?

2. Do we understand our opportunities?

    ◦ What is our understanding of our opportunities?
    ◦ What are the opportunities available for a century?
    ◦ What opportunities do we expect we can exploit in near future? Why?

3. Do we understand the real potential of each of them?

    ◦ Discuss the potential of each of the opportunities available to you.

4. Are we unable to see some opportunities (which our competitors and others in the industry can see)?

    ◦ Identifying the opportunities early is a competitive advantage that gives us strength in the marketplace. Can we identify some of the opportunities, which we have missed but, our competitors and other industry players are enthusiastic about them?
    ◦ What could be the reasons for missing the opportunities?

5. How do we plan to exploit these opportunities?

    ◦ What are our plans to exploit each of the opportunities?

6. Do we have the required resources and plan ready for it?

    ◦ Are we ready with resources to exploit these opportunities?

7. What challenges do we see in these opportunities?

    ◦ What are the challenges associated with each one of these opportunities?
    ◦ How do we plan to deal with them?

8. What action do we need to take to capture these opportunities?

    ◦ What should be our present actions to capture the existing opportunities?

9. What is our method/ process of discovering opportunities?

    ◦ What is our methodology and process for identifying the opportunities in the marketplace?

10. What we did do with the opportunities before?

    ◦ What is our experience with the identification and exploitation of opportunities?

11. Did we exploit them fully?

    ◦ How successful we were before with the identified opportunities?

12. What were the mistakes?

    ◦ What is our learning after those experiences?

13. Did we correct them with feedback?

- How did we improve with the insights from our experiences?

14. What was the result?

   - How much did we improve after bringing the required changes in our organization?

15. What can we do to improve our opportunities discovery?

   - Is there any way that we can improve our identification of opportunities before our competitors?

16. How can we improve to exploit the opportunities?

   - How can we become better at exploiting the opportunities available to us?

17. What can we learn from others inside the industry and outside?

   - What is our analysis of our competitors and other industry players about the identification and exploitation of opportunities?
   - What is our learning?

CHAPTER EIGHT

Does the mission need to be revisited?

1. Are you satisfied with the mission?

    ◦ What is the satisfaction level of the top management, middle management, and employees with the mission and its impact on the organization's performance?

2. Are the other stakeholders connected with the mission?

    ◦ What is the confidence level of other stakeholders with our mission statement?

3. How have the times and trends changed since the time the mission was created?

    ◦ Have the changes in the marketplace and technology affected our mission statement?

4. What our competitors and people in the industry are doing?

    ◦ What is our understanding of our competitors and other industry players in relation to their mission?

5. Are we growing as per our expectations?

- Are we satisfied with our execution and implementation of plans and strategy?

6. What are the reasons if we are not growing?

   - What can be the reasons for our slow growth, both internal and external?

7. What wrong decisions and actions we have taken?

   - What is our understanding of our wrong decisions and actions?
   - How have they affected us?
   - How did we correct ourselves?
   - What was our learning?

8. What was the reason for that?

   - What were the reasons which were responsible for taking those wrong decisions and actions?

9. How the mission has changed over the years?

   - How has our mission statement been modified over the book of the life of the organization?
   - How had it affected our strategy and planning?
   - What positive and negative effects we had on ourselves after the changes?

10. What was the stimulus for it?

    - What were the reasons for bringing the changes in our mission statement?

11. What was the process of recreating the mission?

    - What are the positives followed in changing our mission statement?

12. How does our mission compare with others (in industry and other industries)?

    ◦ What is the strength and weaknesses of our mission in comparison to other industry players?

13. Is it motivating enough?

    ◦ Is our mission statement able to motivate our all stakeholders?
    ◦ Is it able to bring clarity to their decisions and actions?

14. Is it clear enough?

    ◦ Is the mission statement simple and clear for all our stakeholders?

15. Does everyone in the organization understand their goals and responsibilities?

    ◦ Is our mission statement able to define the roles, responsibilities, and objectives of each and everyone in the organization?

An effective mission statement scans the outside environment of business and answers the questions about making a difference, setting new standards of performance, and inspiring commitment.

To support the major question we need to ask cross/sub-questions to understand the challenges and opportunities to inspire innovation. We even need to question the relevance of the mission statement based on the changes in the trends and the behaviors of the market. That is the reason the mission statement should be classic, which is relevant even when the market realities changes and technologies are upgraded. The mission statement should aspire the managers to ask different and relevant questions so that it can produce new insights for inspiring a fresh direction and understanding their business in the market in a new way. It means that the fundamental purpose and the core values of the organization rarely change while technologies, business processes, culture, strategies, structures, methods, and operating practices consistently change. This simply means the difference between "what we stand for"- which stands for the fundamentals of the organization, and "how we do things" - which stands for its processes and tactics, which change with time.

The final objective is to satisfy the customer sent to the markets by doing something new and fresh through innovation.

Question 2- Who Is Our Customer?

The second question is focused on defining the customers, which asks "Who is our customer?" For any organization, the satisfaction of customers is of utmost importance. That is the reason, we need to understand our customers, which starts by defining them in clear words.

2. Who Is Our Customer?

The second question is focused on defining the customers, which asks "Who is our customer?" For any organization, the satisfaction of customers is of utmost importance. That is the reason, we need to understand our customers, which starts by defining them in clear words.

CHAPTER TEN

Our Customers

Social service and nonprofit organizations have two types of customers. **The primary customer** is the person whose life is changed through the work of the organization. Supporting customers are volunteers, members, partners, funders, referral sources, employees, and others who must be satisfied.

Customers are never static; there will be greater or lesser numbers in the groups you serve. Often, the customer is one step ahead of you. So, **you must know your customer**—or quickly get to know them.

It is necessary to constantly learn about your customers as they are neither static nor dormant, they are alive and always changing. **To innovate we need to understand them**, their needs, and their behavior. In many cases, you will need to observe them as several of the requirements will not be clear to them. It can only be identified through relentless observation. Organizations, which understand their customers well, will be able to produce the winning products. In most cases, it will not be a new product, but instead the minute changes in the product, which creates a positive experience for the customer.

In the context of normal business, the primary customers would be our core customers, who buy our products and services, to make our organization successful and to help in improving our products and services. These customers make the firm profitable and innovative. **All the stakeholders of the organization work to satisfy the primary customers.** These customers feel emotionally engaged with the brand of the organization and contribute to improving it.

In the context of normal business, **the supporting customers** are all stakeholders, other than the primary customers of the organization. All the supporting customers work to satisfy the needs and requirements of the primary customers. It is the main reason that the supporting customers understand the primary customers and their needs. They need to feel connected to them. Organizations that can achieve this target, get success in the marketplace. If we look at the history of business then we can find all the successful companies following this principle.

Even with the changing times, this idea remains relevant. This concept is a classic and every time we ponder on it, we find something new in it. It could be a nice start for bringing innovation to the organization.

Who is our customer

Now let us dig deeper into the fundamental question no. 2, which is, 'Who is our customer?' In this section, we will cover a large number of sub-questions, which can help us to understand our customers and other concepts related to them.

The right way to do this section is to first understand the meaning of each question and answer it broadly in your mind. After each question, you should pause for a moment and answer the question in your mind, without writing it down. Do it for each and every question. There could be some questions, which are not relevant to you, and can be skipped. It is up to you to identify the questions relevant to you and answer them sincerely. We can assure you that once the questioning of this section is over, you would know enough about your organization and its customers.

Once you have reached the end of the section, we suggest you come back and again start the questions from the beginning, and repeat the process. You need to understand that only thinking about the answers in the mind is not enough. most of the time it is vague, not clear. Once you write your ideas and understanding down on a piece of paper or digitally, then you have truly answered the question.

Let's move to questions.

Questions

Who is our primary customer?

Define your main customers for whom the organization exists. All the functions of the organization lead to the satisfaction of these customers through products and services.

1. How do we define our customers?

    ◦ We have to clearly define the present definition we have for our customers. Is it clear and complete?
    ◦ Are you missing any element which is required for defining the customer?

2. Can everyone in the organization understand the definition of our customers?

    ◦ Everybody in the organization must understand the similar definition of the customers. We need to check the understanding of our primary customers from different stakeholders of the organization.

3. Do our employees and managers feel connected to customers? If not, why?

    ◦ Without feeling connectivity with customers it would be difficult to serve them through products and services. Is the organization taken efforts to build this type of connectivity?
    ◦ What is the level of connectivity that other employees and managers feel with the customers? Rate on a scale of 10 with 1 as minimum and 10 as maximum.

4. What can we do to enhance customer engagement in our organization?

    ◦ What steps do we need to take to enhance customer engagement in our organization?
    ◦ The more customers are engaged with the organization the better able to serve them by understanding their requirements and needs.

5. What are the challenges to connecting with our primary customers?

    ◦ What are the challenges we are facing to connect with our customers?
    ◦ What steps do we need to take to deal with these challenges?
    ◦ Are we missing any opportunity for a better connection with the customers?

- How can we utilize the present trends and technology to connect better with customers?

6. How our customers are segmented?

   - Do we understand the complete segmentation of our customers?
   - Are we designing customized products and services for them?
   - Are the customers look satisfied with our offerings?

7. What are their geographical locations?

   - What is the location of her customers?
   - Are we efficiently able to reach our customers?
   - Is our distribution and customer support working as per the requirements?

8. How do we understand the behavior of our customers?

   - How are we understanding our customers?
   - How their needs and requirements are changing with time?
   - Are our offerings meeting these changes in needs?
   - What steps do we need to take to connect with them better?

9. How have our predictions about customers played out in the past?

   - How good we are at forecasting our sales?
   - Are our roots keeping pace with the changing trends and needs of the customers?
   - Are we able to keep our customers satisfied and even delighted?
   - What are the problem points?
   - Which area requires better planning and resources?

10. What is the definition of primary customers for our competitors?

   - The market research for the industry and the competitors would provide us with information and new insights about the customers. If we can understand the definition of the primary customer for our competitors we could identify a few areas which we have missed. It would also act as a resource for developing a competitive strategy and understanding the market.

11. How well our competitors are connected with their primary customers?

- This is the second important research for our competitors, to know their connection with their customers. Competitors which are not well connected with their customers cannot be a threat as those companies would lose their strength over time. The competitors who have their customers as advocates can be a big force in the industry in the future. We need to learn from them and their techniques to delight their customers.

12. How has the definition of primary customers changed for us?

- Has the definition of primary customers changed over the years?
- What prompted those changes?
- What was our experience in changing the definition and how it played out?
- What we can learn from it?

13. How has the definition of primary customers changed for our competitors and other organizations in our industry?

- How the definition of the primary customer has changed in our industry?
- For our customers?
- What trends are responsible for bringing those changes in the definition of primary customers?
- What these changes affected our company and its products?)

14. How can we utilize technology & innovative ideas to enhance customer engagement?

- How do we define the technological changes in communication in the last five years?
- How have we utilized this development in technology to connect with our customers better?

- ◦ Where do we lack in this area?
- ◦ What actions do we need to take to enhance our customer engagement by utilizing the latest changes in the marketplace?

15. What market share our primary customers constitute?

- ◦ What is our market share in the marketplace?
- ◦ What is the percentage of customers leaving us?
- ◦ What are the reasons for these customers to leave us?
- ◦ What actions do we need to take to reduce his percentage to the minimum?
- ◦ Which computer is having the maximum market share growth rate?
- ◦ What we can learn from them?

16. How can we enhance or improve our market share?

- ◦ What is the growth rate of our market share?
- ◦ What we can do to enhance this market share?
- ◦ Is there anything that we can learn from our competitors and other players in the industry?

17. What changes would be required in the organization to achieve the target?

- ◦ How do we define our organization at the present moment?
- ◦ Is our organization changing as per the definition of our mission and the changes in the marketplace?
- ◦ How do we define our company's ideal self?
- ◦ What changes are required in our organization to move towards its ideal self?

18. What training would our managers and employees need to be part of the required change?

- ◦ What new skills and competencies would be required to support the required changes in the organization?
- ◦ How the regular training programs should be designed so that our managers and employees remain up to date in their skills and

knowledge?
- ◦ How do we calculate our return on investment in training?
- ◦ Is it appreciable enough?
- ◦ How can we make it better?

CHAPTER ELEVEN

Who are our supporting customers?

1. How do we define our supporting customers?

    ○ What is the definition of our supporting customers?
    ○ How do we segment them?
    ○ In what way do our supporting customers provide strength to our organization?
    ○ Are we able to manage them well?

2. Are our supporting customers satisfied?

    ○ How do we define the meaning of satisfaction for our supporting customers?
    ○ What is the satisfaction level of our supporting customers?
    ○ How article create their satisfaction level?
    ○ What efforts we are doing to ensure their satisfaction?)

3. What is the satisfaction level of our supporting customers in relation to the industry standard?

    ○ How do we stand in comparison to other industry players in the satisfaction level of our supporting customers?
    ○ How can we improve our position by raising the satisfaction level of our supporting customers?
    ○ What can we learn from other industry players who have high satisfaction levels with their supporting customers?

4. How can we enhance the satisfaction level of our supporting customers?

   - What challenges do we have to raise the satisfaction level of our supporting customers?
   - How can we deal with these challenges?
   - How can we make the high satisfaction level of our supporting customers a priority in our organization?

5. What can be the reasons that the satisfaction level of the customers would go down?

   - What would be the reasons responsible for pulling down the satisfaction level of our customers both primary and supporting?
   - How severe are these reasons?
   - What are we doing to deal with these reasons?

6. What is the commitment level of the supporting customers towards the organization?

   - Are we able to maintain a high level of commitment from our supporting customers?
   - What are the reasons for their low commitment?
   - What steps can we take to raise the commitment level of our supporting customers, towards our organization?

7. What can be the reasons for the specific commitment level?

   - How do we define the present relationship of our organization with the supporting customers?
   - How can they be more loyal to the organization?

8. What are the different needs of different supporting customers?

   - What are their needs?
   - Are we fulfilling those needs?
   - How can we understand their needs better?

9. How much value each segment of supporting customers are adding to our business?

    - Do we understand the value addition by each customer segment of supporting customers?
    - What are the obstructions to value addition?
    - What can we do to enhance that value addition?

10. Are our supporting customers working in unison to create synergy? If not why?

    - How are supporting customers working together?
    - Is the communication and workflow between them smooth?
    - How can we improve it to make them more productive and efficient?

11. How can we improve the synergy of supporting customers?

    - How can we utilize the latest technologies and techniques to improve the synergy of the supporting customers?
    - How can we manage them better?

12. How can we bring innovation and improvement processes to make them more productive?

    - How can we innovate better?
    - How our supporting customers can add value to innovation?
    - What changes we will need to bring in our operations, planning, and strategy to become more productive overall?

13. Where do we stand on the productivity scale in the industry in the world market?

    - How productive we are?
    - How this productivity level compares in the industry and among the competitors?
    - What can we learn from other players to improve productivity?
    - How can we enhance our productivity?

CHAPTER TWELVE

How will our customers change?

1. What are the latest trends in the marketplace?

   - Specify the latest trends which are affecting the marketplace. These could be the actions of competitors, technological changes, political forces, and changes in customer needs. Our business strategy should be based on our mission and the changes in the marketplace.

2. How the thinking pattern of the customers have changed over time?

   - How well do we understand our customers?
   - How they have changed over a period of time?
   - What are the reasons or the forces responsible for these changes?

3. How technology is contributing to these changes?

   - What effect technology is having on our business and industry?
   - How fast technology is changing?
   - How are the competitors utilizing it?
   - What can we do to make technology one of our strengths?

4. How our customers are reacting to these changes?

   - Different customers react in different ways to the changes in the marketplace.

- How our different customer segments are reacting to the changes and trends of the marketplace?
- How can we remain ahead of our competitors in meeting the changing needs of our customers?
- How can we enhance our profitability during these changes?

5. Do we understand these changes? How have we responded to these changes in the past?

- How are we able to exploit these changes in the past?
- What can we learn from those experiences?
- What can we do to enhance our understanding and prediction of these changes?
- How can we be more proactive?

6. How successful we were (in the past) to change the organization based on customer changes?

- Specify the successes and failures while changing the organization based on the market forces.
- Specify your learnings from these experiences.
- How has your process of bringing change to the organization improved?
- How can you ensure a high level of value addition in the next phase of organizational change?

7. What is the process of understanding market changes?

- How good and fast we are in understanding the market changes?
- How is it in comparison to our competitors and other players in the industry?
- How can we improve our process of understanding in predicting market changes?

8. How successful our competitors are to react to these changes?

- What has been the strategy of our competitors to exploit the market changes?

- What can we learn from them?

9. Are we proactive or reactive to the changes?

   - What do we call ourselves proactive or reactive to the changes in the marketplace?
   - How can we be more proactive?

10. How are competitors behave in these changes?

    - Which are the strong and weak areas of our competitors?
    - How can we utilize the market changes to enhance our market share and brand image?

11. Are these changes bring opportunities or challenges for us? Why?

    - How do we consider the changes in the market, threats, or opportunities? Why?
    - How can we convert the challenges into opportunities?
    - How can we manage our risk better?

12. Can we utilize these changes as an opportunity for us? How can you do that?

    - All the winning companies convert any threat or challenge into opportunities. They utilize the complex changes in the marketplace to gain market share and become stronger. How can we become that winning company?

13. How the size of primary customers is increasing or decreasing based on these changes?

    - How have these market changes affected our market share in the past?
    - Has we analyzed our weaknesses in depth?
    - What changes do we need to bring to our organization to exploit the market she is better?

14. How it is affecting our market share?

  ◦ How our present organization design, processes, and structure are affecting our ability to deal with market changes?
  ◦ Are we able to keep pace with the changing demands of the customers?

15. How strong we are in innovation?

  ◦ How well they have innovated in the past?
  ◦ How successful we have been in our innovation are the marketplace?
  ◦ What has been our learning about innovation?
  ◦ Have we implemented that learning in our organization?
  ◦ How can we improve our process of innovation?

16. Does our innovation are liked by our customers?

  ◦ Have our innovations been appreciated by our customers, both primary and supporting?
  ◦ Has he taken help from our customers to innovate better?
  ◦ How can we incorporate the ideas of our customers and our future products and services?

17. How often we have created successful products and services for our customers?

  ◦ How successful we have been in the past in introducing new person services?
  ◦ What has been our learning?
  ◦ What is our plan for the future?
  ◦ How can we improve it?

18. What is the process of innovation in our company? Is it effective? Why?

  ◦ What is the present process of innovation in our organization?
  ◦ How it can be better than other industry players?

19. Are we satisfied with the innovation processes of our organization?

- ◦ What is our satisfaction level with the innovation of our organization?
- ◦ Is our innovation serving the needs of the market?
- ◦ Are our customers satisfied with our products?
- ◦ Where we are lacking?
- ◦ How can we improve it?

In these questions, we try to bring out a clear definition for our customers so that we could satisfy them with our efforts and innovation.

Strangely, most corporate leaders fail to define their customers. It means that they do not understand their customers and that's a reason the primary customers are not the center of their attention. In some cases, it has been found that some of the corporate leaders have some vague idea about their customers which at best confuses them and the organization. In these cases, everybody has a different definition of the primary customers, which is not only pathetic but dangerous. It should be the primary responsibility of the corporate senior management to define their primary customers and the ways to satisfy them. Then they have to communicate their understanding to other stakeholders of the organization. Without the feeling of connection with customers, other employees and managers cannot work in synergy to create great products and serve their customers better.

Answering the question 'Who is our customer?' provides the basis for determining what customers value, defining your results, and developing the plan. Once we are clear about our primary customers then we can focus our attention to understand and satisfy their needs and requirements.

Primary and supporting customers for NGOs and Non-Profits.

In the case of NGOs and nonprofit organizations, they have to differentiate between their primary and supporting customers. These organizations exist to serve their primary customers, people who are getting the benefits out of the efforts of the organization. But in this case, the supporting customers have the power to say no to your proposals and offers. For example, the government is the supporting customer for nonprofit organizations and NGOs, and they can reject an offer or a proposal. We need to clearly understand the behavior and thinking process of the supporting customers before proposing anything to them. We need to understand their objectives and the market forces in which they operate.

The question about the needs of the customers can only be answered by engaging with customers and observing them at required places and conditions. For example, to understand the needs of the customer for a personal vehicle the new generation can be understood by the difficulties they are facing while they are driving their car, looking for parking space, and understanding their specific variable and fixed costs, design choices, personal and professional needs. Customers cannot answer all of these questions but expert marketers and researchers can identify their implicit needs which customers are not able to express in words. We also need to understand that customers are constantly changing and updating their opinions. The requirements, goals, and wants evolve with time and environment. To understand the concept let's take the example of a mobile manufacturing company, which has become a highly complex, competitive but profitable business in recent times. The creators of future products will need to understand the different geographies, demographics, genders, and challenges faced by people, which mobile phones can resolve. They also must understand the upcoming technologies which will be utilized to develop future forms and understand their integration with other technologies. In addition to these the needs of the customer must be kept in mind. It is to be understood that the needs of today can be modified by changing trends and behaviors of the customers.

Satisfying supporting customers

in addition to delighting the primary customers, we need to understand and satisfy our supporting customers. An NGO or nonprofit organization could be termed a collaborator or partner. They are the essential element of providing the services to the primary customers and they can enhance or degrade it. NGOs that work for education may have government officials, publishers, financiers, teachers, volunteers, community leaders, and many other people and organizations as they are supporting customers. These supporting customers help to support the services provided by the organization so that it remains smooth and of high quality. Without the efforts of the supporting customers, the primary customers cannot be served.

That is the reason we need to know and understand our supporting customers and make every effort to keep them motivated and productive.

Question 3–What Does the Customer Value?

The most important question out of five questions.

CHAPTER THIRTEEN

What Does the Customer Value?

What the customer value can be considered as the most important question out of five questions. Every organization must figure out, what their customers value and what they are willing to pay for it. It means understanding their needs, wants, and aspirations. This question is not easy question to answer.

Ironically many businesses fail to answer this question, the reasons may vary:

- they do not consider it as important
- they do not know the process of answering it
- they do not have the required resources to get the data and information
- they do not want to put the required resources for the research
- even if they have the data, they do not know the ways to transform it into information and insights.
- They have a process in place, but they are doing it half-heartedly, leading to bad insights about customer value.

It is important to know about what customer value, before focusing on innovation, as without the relevant information you will not be able to innovate. But, if you focus on getting the right information about customer value, and the behaviors of the market, then it would lead to high dividends while developing products and services for the customers. We will be able to create products that will be appreciated by customers and would gain acceptance in the market in a minimal time.

Customers also respect organizations, which work hard toward understanding their needs and requirements, so that they can develop the right products for them. In today's time, several good companies focus on getting feedback from customers as a way to consistently improve themselves and their offerings. They want to understand the problems faced by the customers and identify solutions for them. The important point here is to be sincere about listening to customers.

Thanks to social networking and communication technologies, organizations now have the means to connect with their customers in a whole new way. They can work with the customers to develop products and improve their offerings over a period of time.

These days, most corporate leaders know about the necessity to focus on customers to understand their needs for innovation. But, what about the needs and requirements about which the customers do not know? According to Steve Jobs, the past CEO of Apple, it is very hard to design a perfect product for the customers by asking them, as most of the customers do not know what they want until you show it to them. For designing the product, the managers should not stop at the most obvious or simplest solution, instead, they should help customers to understand the realities of their ideal experience by digging deeper, framing, reframing, and exploring different angles.

To get success, organizations must work very closely with the customers, as it will be a self-discovery even for the customers about their needs.

Now let us dig deeper into the fundamental question 3, which is, 'What does customer value?' In this section, we will cover a large number of sub-questions, which can help us to understand what our customers' value, and other concepts related to it.

The right way to do this section is to first understand the meaning of each question and answer it broadly in your mind. After each question, you should pause for some time to answer the question in your mind, without writing it down. Do it for each and every question. There could be some questions, which are not relevant to you, and can be skipped. It is up to you to identify the questions relevant to you and answer them sincerely. We can assure you that once the questioning of this section is over, you would know enough about your organization and the required value as defined by its customers.

Once you have reached the end of the section, we suggest you come back and again start the questions from the beginning, and repeat the process. You need to understand that only thinking about the answers in the mind is not enough, most of the time it is vague, and not clear. Once you write your ideas and understanding down on a piece of paper or digitally, then you have truly answered the question.

Let's move to questions.

What do we believe our primary and supporting customers value?

1. What is it that you do especially well that you are uniquely suited to provide to your customers?

    - Why do our customers appreciate us?
    - Why are they with us?
    - How competitors are trying to snatch our customers from us?
    - What are we doing about it?
    - Do we feel confident about keeping our customers happy and satisfied with our products and services?

2. How can you exceed the standards set by your competition?

    - Do we understand the standards set by industry players in the marketplace?
    - What is the perception in the marketplace about the industry players, including us?
    - What can we do to exceed the expectations of the marketplace/to delight them?

3. How do we define value for our customers?

    - What is the definition of value according to us?
    - How have we defined this definition- the process?
    - How confident we are about this definition?

4. What customer's requirements/ needs are getting fulfilled?

    - What are the specific demand and needs of the customers which are getting fulfilled by our products and services?
    - Do customers agree with us regarding the satisfaction level?

5. How do customers define value?

   - How the value is defined by our primary customers?
   - How is the value defined by our supporting customers?
   - What is the process of defining these definitions?
   - Do our competitors have similar definitions?
   - How these definitions are helping us to create products and services?
   - How do we bring change to our products and services?

6. What is the difference between these defined values?

   - What is the difference between the definition of value by us and by our customers?
   - What are the reasons for these differences?
   - What actions do we need to take to synchronize both definitions?)

7. What is the difference in perceiving the value of our products and services for primary and supporting customers? Why?

   - What are the reasons for the difference in the definition of value by primary and supporting customers?

8. How do we plan to solve it?

   - What actions do we need to take to synchronize the definition of value for all, with primary customers as a source?
   - Is there anything that our customers want but are not aware of it yet?
   - How can we test the new ideas?

9. What is our process of understanding the definition of value for our customers?

   - What is our present process of understanding our customers and their definition of value?
   - Is there any way to improve it?

10. How our competitors are learning about it?

- ◦ What our Competitors are doing in understanding the value definition of the customers?
- ◦ What can we learn from them?

11. What are the flaws in our method? Can there be a better method?

- ◦ How can our present methodology of understanding the value of customers become better?
- ◦ What actions do we need to take for that?

12. How do we record these insights?

- ◦ What is the process of capturing insights from the customers?
- ◦ How do we process these insights to get ideas about new products?

13. What do we do with these insights?

- ◦ Do we have a dedicated team and experts to understand our primary customers?
- ◦ What methodology do they use to generate fresh ideas?
- ◦ Are we satisfied with it?

14. Have these insights added to our strength previously? Why or why not?

- ◦ What is our experience of generating and utilizing the insights of the customers previously?
- ◦ What is our learning from it?
- ◦ How can we utilize it better?

15. What is the customer's satisfaction level with our products?

- ◦ Are our customers satisfied with our products and services?
- ◦ What is the satisfaction level?
- ◦ What are their feedback and complaints?
- ◦ What are we doing presently to enhance their satisfaction level?
- ◦ What should we do to delight our customers?

16. How does it compare with others in the industry?

- How our efforts to connect and delight our customers are in comparison to our competitors?
- Is there any need for improvement?
- How can we do that?

17. How can we enhance this customer's satisfaction?

- Can we think with a fresh mind, just like a new company, the ways to satisfy our customers?

CHAPTER FOURTEEN

What knowledge do we need to gain from our customers?

What data, information, and insights are we getting from our customers? How are we extracting knowledge out of it?

1. What information we would need from the market?

    ◦ Where are we lacking in market knowledge?
    ◦ How can we get that information?

2. How the data will be generated?

    ◦ What would be the process of collecting the data about the market?
    ◦ What would be the process of collecting the information about our customers?
    ◦ How can we become more efficient in the collection of data?

3. How this data will be converted to the information?

    ◦ How the collected data is being processed in our organization?
    ◦ Are we able to generate the required information from the data?

4. How we will generate insights?

    ◦ How do we get insights about the market and customers presently?
    ◦ How can we improve the quality of our insights?

5. How these ideas will be used?

- How do we use the market and customer insights?
- How can these insights help us in better decisions?
- How our competitors are generating and utilizing customer and market information?

6. What information we are getting what customers now?

    - Explain the type and the format in which we are getting information now. Is it working for us?
    - Is there a better way to get the information more efficiently?

7. What is the process of getting that information?

    - What is our process of processing the information and data to get insights from it?
    - Are these insights helping us to make better decisions?
    - If not, how can we get better insights from our data?

8. Are we getting complete or incomplete information?

    - Is the data we are collecting from the market and customers, complete?
    - Are we able to generate the required information from it?
    - Are our decisions based on the generated insights effective or not?
    - What can we do to fill the gap in data and information?

9. How can we make the process of getting information about the customers better?

    - Can we identify better ways to generate data and collect information about the market and customers?
    - What is our process for collecting information about our competitors?
    - Are we satisfied with it?
    - Can we make it better?

10. Can we learn from others in the industry or other industries about getting data about the customer?

- ◦ Identify other players in the industry and find their systems for collecting data about customers.
- ◦ What is different they are doing?
- ◦ What can we learn from them?

11. Are we utilizing the information we are getting from the marketing?

- ◦ Are we effectively using the data and information generated by the marketing department?
- ◦ Do we completely trust the data generated by the marketing team?
- ◦ What is the return on investment for us?
- ◦ How can we make the ROI of marketing better?

12. How has this information improved our offerings in the market?

- ◦ How have we implemented market and customer insights into our products and services?
- ◦ How has it helped us to create customized products and services for our customers?
- ◦ Are we able to raise the satisfaction level of our customers?
- ◦ If not, what are we lacking?
- ◦ How can we improve it?

How will I participate in gaining this knowledge?

What role the different segments of our organization should play to understand the customer and they are expected value from us?

1. How do we interact with our customers?

   - How are we interacting with our customers?
   - What is the point of contact with our customers?
   - How do we communicate information to our customers?
   - Is it effective?
   - If not, how can we improve it?

2. Are we getting all the required information about the customers?

   - Is there any area in which we are lacking in getting information about our customers and their satisfaction level with our products?

3. How are our competitors getting information about the customers?

   - How our competitors are collecting information about the customers and the market?
   - How are they processing their information?
   - What is the quality of their insights?

4. Can we learn anything from them?

   - Are there decisions better than ours?

- ◦ What can we learn from them?

5. How can we use technology to connect better with other customers?

   - ◦ How did communication technology change over the past few years?
   - ◦ Are we utilizing its power?
   - ◦ Which systems, methods, and technologies can help us to connect with our customers better and to understand them?

6. How can customers help us in developing and designing better products and services?

   - ◦ What type of communication we should be having with our customers to understand their needs?
   - ◦ How can we capture their insights, advice, and suggestions about our products and services?
   - ◦ How can we utilize those ideas to design and develop better products?

7. How do we interact with our customers?

   - ◦ How do we connect with our customers?
   - ◦ How effective is our present method?

8. Are we getting all the required information about the customers?

   - ◦ What type of information are we generating with our interaction with customers?
   - ◦ What is the generated information as per the requirements of the design team?

9. How are our competitors getting information about the customers?

   - ◦ What is our understanding of other industry players for generating information about the market?
   - ◦ What are the strengths and weaknesses of their methods?

10. Can we learn anything from them?

- What is our learning from the analysis of our competitors?
- What ideas can we utilize to make our systems better?

11. How can we use technology to connect better with other customers?

- Which communication technology we can use to connect with our customers in a better way?
- In what ways the new system would be better for us?

12. How can customers help us in developing and designing better products and services?

- What is the best way to involve customers in designing our new products?
- How can we capture and utilize the feedback of customers to improve our present products?

Question 4- What Are Our Results?

How much do you know about the results to achieve?

CHAPTER SIXTEEN

What are our results?

Every initiative or action which we take should have clearly defined results. That is the purpose of the whole action. Results are also an important part of providing feedback about our actions by analyzing the achieved results and the expected results. It is also important to evaluate the results through both quantitative and qualitative means. Both measures support each other as a means of analyzing the results.

In the case of nonprofits, the results are the changes in the lives of the people and their conditions of living, for whom they exist. These results should be measured in both quantitative and qualitative terms. The leaders of the NGO or a nonprofit organization must ask the question "do we produce results that are sufficiently outstanding for us, to justify putting our resources in this area?" If we are affirmative and confident about the answer to this question, then we are on the right track to achieving the results.

For other organizations, even if we do not have enough authority to change the results, asking this question would help us in giving new perspectives, and open new doors of ideas for us to explore. This can be a new way to innovate and satisfy customers in fresh ways. It is important to note that the results achieved must be meaningful, sensible, and have value for everyone involved in the process.

If we can answer this question well, then it becomes easy for us to answer the fifth and last question "what is our plan?" We can use achieved results as a tool for learning, getting feedback, and refining ourselves to produce better results next time.

This must be the goal of managing to put the resources and energy in the right direction, for the future success of the organization. It is the responsibility of the leaders to take accountability, and improve management to get the desired results. To achieve the results, leaders must learn from their mistakes by admitting failures and blunders. To create real impact, we need to constantly introspect, measure, learn and keep improving. Leadership requires assessing what should be strengthened and what should be abandoned. It is said that the abandonment of activities that are no longer productive must be the priority, but it is most difficult to achieve, as people resist it.

What are our results?

Now let us dig deeper into the fundamental question 4, which is, 'What are our results?' In this section, we will cover a large number of sub-questions, which can help us to understand the results to be achieved by us and other concepts related to it.

The right way to do this section is to first understand the meaning of each question and answer it broadly in your mind. After each question, you should pause for some time and answer the question in your mind, without writing it down. Do it for each and every question. There could be some questions, which are not relevant to you, and can be skipped. It is up to you to identify the questions relevant to you and answer them sincerely. We can assure you that once the questioning of this section is over, you would know enough about your organization and the results to be achieved.

Once you have reached the end of the section, we suggest you come back and again start the questions from the beginning, and repeat the process. You need to understand that only thinking about the answers in the mind is not enough, most of the time it is vague, and not clear. Once you write your ideas and understanding down on a piece of paper or digitally, then you have truly answered the question.

Let's move to questions.

How do we define results? How do we measure success?

1. What are our results?

    - Write a clear definition of the results, which you are trying to achieve.
    - How can we make sure that the definition of the result is correct?
    - Are these results in synchronization with our mission statement?

2. Do all stakeholders agree with the definition of the result?

- What is the definition of results according to different stakeholders of the organization?
- What is the difference between these definitions?
- What is the reason for these differences? How we can bring all the definitions in synchronization?

3. How these results are related to customer satisfaction?

   - Are these results enough to satisfy the needs of our customers?
   - Are these results delivering the required value asked by the customers?

4. Are we getting the desired results? Why?

   - Are we able to achieve the required results?
   - What are the reasons for not being able to achieve the required results?
   - How can we rectify it?

5. What can we do to get better results?

   - Can we identify different ways to enhance the quality of our results?

6. How do we compare to the industry benchmark in getting results?

   - We do we stand in comparison to another industry benchmark in operations, marketing, and other areas?
   - Where do we lack and what other reasons for it?
   - How can we improve in each of these areas?

7. Are we satisfied with the results?

   - What is our satisfaction level with achieving results?
   - Is there any way to improve our satisfaction level?

8. How do we measure them?

   - Are these results delivering profitability to the organization?

- Are these results able to satisfy our customers?

9. What are its quantitative and qualitative parameters of it?

   - How do we measure our results in both qualitative and quantitative ways?

10. Is our understanding of results satisfactory?

    - Does everyone in the organization is able to describe results properly and clearly?
    - Is everyone in the organization can connect their work profile with the results to be achieved?

11. Are we productive in getting results?

    - How do we measure our productivity quantitatively?
    - Where do we stand in productivity in comparison to the industry standard?
    - How can we surpass the industry standard?

12. How can we become more productive?

    - Which are the weak areas in our productivity?
    - How we can improve upon them?
    - Which are our strong areas in our productivity?
    - How can we strengthen them?

13. Do these results make business sense?

    - In what way do our results add value to our business?
    - Is our quest for results would deliver growth for our organization?

14. Do everyone in the organization understand these results and work for them? Are employees connected to the results?

    - How the information flows in our organization?

- Is everybody is able to understand the communication in their context?
- How has the definition of results affected the quality of work by our employees?

15. Do we produce results that are sufficiently outstanding for us to justify putting our resources in this area?

- Are clear about the direction we are taking for our organization?
- Do we have clearly defined medium-term and long-term goals?
- Are we confident about the return on investment for these goals?

CHAPTER SEVENTEEN

Are we successful?

- How do we define success for our organization?
- How are employees define success for themselves?
- Are both the definition of success in synchronization?
- If not, how can we correct it?

1. Are we satisfied?

   ◦ Do our managers and other employees of the organization feel satisfied working for the organization?
   ◦ What is the satisfaction level on a scale of 10 with 10 as the maximum and 1 as the minimum?

2. What is the reason for it?

   ◦ If our satisfaction level is low the work would be the reason?
   ◦ What corrective actions do we need to take?

3. How does our success compare with the industry?

   ◦ How successful we are in comparison to other industry players?

4. How do we compare with the competitors?

   ◦ If we compare ourselves with our main competitors which are the major differences we would identify?
   ◦ Which are our strong and weak areas?
   ◦ How can we strengthen our strong areas and manage our weak areas?

5. What can we do to become better?

    ◦ What actions do we need to take to become better in every area? What is our learning from the industry analysis?)

6. Is our understanding of success correct? Why?

    ◦ Is our present way of thinking and acting giving us success?
    ◦ Where is our weakness?
    ◦ How can we improve our thinking process and execution?

7. How can we make this definition more relevant?

    ◦ Does our definition of success include all important elements?
    ◦ Do we need to redefine our definition of success?
    ◦ What process do we need to follow to rework the definition of success?

8. Do our stakeholders consider themselves successful? Why?

    ◦ Does our definition of success include all our stakeholders?
    ◦ How our success is making them successful?

9. Are they motivated?

    ◦ Are all our stakeholders feel motivated to work and be connected with the organization?
    ◦ In which areas we can feel the weakness?
    ◦ What actions do we need to take to correct it?

10. What can we do to motivate our stakeholders?

    ◦ What special efforts are we taking presently to keep our stakeholders energized and motivated?
    ◦ How can we improve it?

11. How positive are our stakeholders about the future of the organization?

- ◦ What we use different stakeholders have about the organization?
- ◦ What do they feel about the future of the organization?
- ◦ What suggestions do they have for the growth and enhancement of the strength of the organization?

12. How has our success level changed over the past five years (how successful we have been in the past five years)?

- ◦ What is our analysis of the performance of the organization in the past five years?
- ◦ What is the performance of the industry and other competitors?
- ◦ What actions do we need to take to lead the industry in the coming years?

13. How can we sustain success?

- ◦ What is our sustainability plan?
- ◦ What are our risks?
- ◦ How would we manage those risks?

CHAPTER EIGHTEEN

How should we define results?

1. What are our results?

    ◦ What results are we getting presently?
    ◦ Are these results as per the plans and expectations?
    ◦ Where are the gaps?

2. Does everyone in the organization understand these results?

    ◦ Does everyone in the organization understand their contribution to these results?
    ◦ Do they have suggestions to improve these results?
    ◦ How can we capture these suggestions?
    ◦ How can we analyze and implement them?

3. Do employees and managers know their responsibilities for getting these results?

    ◦ Are the responsibility clearly defined and divided among the managers and employees?
    ◦ Do they understand those responsibilities?
    ◦ Are they competent enough to perform well on these responsibilities?

4. Are they satisfactorily working to get these results?

- Are we satisfied with the performance of our managers and employees?
- Are they able to achieve their goals successfully?
- What is our understanding of the problems in the organization for these areas?

5. Are managers and employees connected to these results and are motivated to achieve them?

   - What is the motivation level of our managers?
   - Are they able to transfer the motivation to their teams?
   - Is this motivation delivering results?

6. How has the definition of resources changed over time?

   - What is the definition of resources for us?
   - How has the definition of resources changed over a period of time?
   - What were the reasons for these changes?
   - Are we able to provide the required resources without any difficulties?
   - What are the challenges in providing resources?

7. How is the definition of results compared with our competitors?

   - What is the difference between the goals of our organization and that of our competitors?

8. What are the reasons for the difference, if any?

   - What is the thought process of our competitors to have a different definition of results?

9. Can we improve the definition of results in any way?

   - Do we need to rework on the definition of our goals and results to be achieved?

10. Are we confident about achieving the results successfully every time?

- What is our confidence level in our competencies and skills in meeting our goals?

11. Are our customers happy with our results?

   - Are these goals in synchronization with the needs of the customers?
   - How have the market changes affected our definition of results in the past?

12. Are we able to have a strong position in the market with these results?

   - Are our goals ambitious and stretched?
   - How our results would help us to achieve a strong position in the market?

CHAPTER NINETEEN

What we must strengthen or abandon?

1. What is our SWOT analysis?

   - Do the strength, weakness, opportunities, and threats analysis.
   - Strengths and weaknesses are internal to the organization while opportunities and threats are outside of the organization and are not in our control.

2. What strengths are the most important ones?

   - Which are our unique distances which create differentiation in the marketplace?
   - Which strengths allow us to retain our customers and attract new ones?

3. How can we strengthen them?

   - What actions do we need to take to strengthen our position in the marketplace?
   - How can we develop new strengths?

4. What are the areas and processes, which are not adding any value?

   - Which are the areas of our actions not adding value to our growth and success?
   - How can we enhance the value proposition of these areas?

5. Can we replace them with something more productive?

    - How can we be more productive?
    - In which areas do we need to improve?

6. What resources we would require for these efforts?

    - What would be required to bring these changes?
    - What actions do we need to take to arrange these resources?

7. What managerial efforts would be required?

    - What skills and competencies would be required?
    - What type of training for managers and employees would be required?

8. What are the risks?

    - What are the challenges we would be facing?
    - Do we understand our risks well?
    - Are we ready to deal with them?

9. How we will manage the risks?

    - How can we deal with each one of the risks?
    - What is our risk management strategy?

10. How are changes in the markets affecting us?

    - How the market trends have affected us in the past?
    - How did we utilize them to gain strength?
    - What is our learning from those experiences?
    - What are the major changes now in the marketplace?
    - How can we utilize them to gain strength?

11. How technology is affecting us?

    - How has technology changed in the past five years?

- How we were able to utilize technology in the past?

12. How can we utilize the changes in the market and technology?

    - What should be our strategy to get opportunities from these changes in the market and technology?

13. Are we satisfied with our market share?

    - What is our present market share?
    - How has it grown in the past five years?
    - What is our strategy to grow it further?

14. Does our image in the marker acceptable/respectable?

    - How can we know about the views of the market and our customers about our products and brand?
    - What is our brand image in the market?
    - What efforts have we taken in the past to strengthen our brand equity?
    - What has been our learning?

15. How can we improve it?

    - What actions do we need to take to strengthen our brand and image in the market?

16. What can we learn from our competitor's mistakes?

    - What is our understanding of the actions taken by our competitors and other industry players to enhance their brand image?
    - What can we learn from them?

Question 5- What Is Our Plan?

The plan and strategy.

Planning is the process to design a plan to achieve a certain objective and the actions we need to take for it.

What Is Our Plan?

Everything is changing very fast which includes markets, customer needs, and technology. In addition to these government regulations, the political environment and market forces are also constantly shifting. All of these changes are putting a lot of pressure on organizations and their managers. That is the reason to have a clearly defined plan for execution.

At the core of a plan, there lies the organization's purpose and the future direction it is going to take. A good plan would incorporate the organization's mission, vision, goals, objectives, financials, and execution plan. Without getting clarity in this area, we cannot be clear about the direction in which we are moving, or how we are going to achieve our goals.

This is the self-assessment process to develop a plan, which is in synchronization with the organization's purpose, and the future direction it is going to take.

Sometimes, it is necessary to review the mission, due to changing times, market realities, and customer needs. To review the mission, we must answer three questions:

1. **what is our purpose?**

   a. The direction we are taking and the goals we need to achieve.

2. **Why do we do what we do?**

   a. The reasons for our actions.

3. **What, in the end, do we want to be remembered for?**

   a. What legacy do we want to leave?

If we can answer these questions honestly then we would have a thorough understanding of the relevance of our mission statement, and the need for any changes or modifications. That could also be the starting point of innovation, as it will give us a different perspective. Many managers do not want to change their mission, because it requires a lot of responsibility and big changes in the organization. They want to keep working on an outdated mission, without understanding the consequences, which could be detrimental to the organization.

Based on the mission we have to develop long-term goals and a plan to achieve those goals. Long-term goals can be broken down into medium-term and short-term goals so that suitable plans can be developed to achieve them.

Understanding and utilizing the concept of goals is an important part of organizational growth. The reasons can be:

- If we do not understand the goals, and we set them wrong, then it is going to take us in the wrong direction, wasting our resources and energy.
- If our goals are contradictory, then again it will not lead us to any sensible results.
- If we are making too many goals, then it's going to stretch us too thin, wasting our resources and energy on irrelevant tasks, without producing anything of value.

The number of goals to be achieved should be few, not too many. If we have more than five goals, then it means that we have no goals, as we will not be able to focus on any of the goals. It is the responsibility of the goals to make it clear, where to focus the resources for results. That is how a serious and growth-oriented organization behaves. The fundamental goal is the mission of the organization. The goals of the organization define its future, as it allows it to focus on a specific aim, build strengths, take risks, and exploit opportunities to get the desired service.

Many managers wrongly think about focusing only on short-term term goals, while ignoring long-term goals. It is to be understood by these managers that the short-term goals must flow from the long-term goals, which in turn flows from the mission of the organization. When everything is in perfect synchronization, then other sources of the organization would be better used, to get the results and achieve growth for the organization. It can be said that for the short-term interest of the organization focus on the long-term goals.

The management must always ask a question about the direction in which the goals are taking the organization. We must ask "Is an objective leading us toward our basic long-range goal, or is it going to sidetrack us, divert us or make us lose sight of our aims?" The objectives are "the specific and measurable levels of achievement, that move the organization toward its goals."

Following the right process of developing the plan for the right goals and objectives, will help us to target the innovation efforts in the right direction, for achieving the mission of the organization.

Do we have a clear plan?

Now let us dig deeper into the fundamental question 5, which is, 'What is our plan?' In this section, we will cover a large number of sub-questions, which can help us to understand our plans, strategy, and other concepts related to it.

The right way to do this section is to first understand the meaning of each question and answer it broadly in your mind. After each question, you should pause for some time to answer the question in your mind, without writing it down. Do it for each and every question. There could be some questions, which are not relevant to you, and can be skipped. It is up to you to identify the questions relevant to you and answer them sincerely. We can assure you that once the questioning of this section is over, you would know enough about your organization and its strategy and planning.

Once you have reached the end of the section, we suggest you come back and again start the questions from the beginning, and repeat the process. You need to understand that only thinking about the answers in the mind is not enough, most of the time it is vague, and not clear. Once you write your ideas and understanding down on a piece of paper or digitally, then you have truly answered the question.

Let's move to questions.

Should the mission be changed?

1. How have the market trends changed over a period of time?

- How have market trends changed in the past five years?
- What was the reaction to these changes?
- How successful we were to deal with these changes in the marketplace?

2. How have the customers' choices changed in the past few years?

   - What are the reasons responsible for changing the needs of the customers in the past five years?
   - Are we successfully meeting the evolving needs of the customers?

3. How has technology affected us?

   - How have the changes in technology been utilized by us?
   - How has it given us strength and made us better?

4. How these changes have impacted our mission?

   - How has our mission changed in the past 10 years?
   - What were the major reasons to bring about these changes?
   - How has it affected our strategy and decisions?

5. Is it still relevant or do we need to change it?

   - What is our understanding of our mission?
   - Is it pulling in the right direction or not?
   - If not, what actions do we need to take to modify our mission so that it could lead us toward growth and success?

6. Why do we think it requires change?

   - What are the reasons responsible for convincing us to mission change?

7. What could be the broad new direction of our organization?

   - What should be the new direction our organization should be taking?
   - What should be our goals and results to be achieved?

8. Is this new direction relevant for the long-term growth of the organization?

   - How would our new understanding of our direction and goals help us to achieve long-term growth for the organization?

9. What are our risks?

   - What would be the risks in the new direction and strategy?

10. How can we manage these risks?

    - What should be our risk strategy to manage the expected problems?

11. How has the mission changed for our competitors?

    - Have there been any changes in the missions of our competitors?
    - What are the reasons for it?

12. How is it working out for them?

    - How have the mission changes affected our competitors?
    - How they were able to deal with the challenges?

13. How has the mission changed for other players in the industry?

    - How have the changes in the marketplace affected other players in the industry?

14. How has our mission changed in the past for us?

    - What effects did the mission changes have on us?

15. What was our experience?

    - What is our understanding of the challenges and difficulties after changing the mission of the organization?

16. What can we learn from it?

   ◦ What is our learning from the previous incidences of mission changes?
   ◦ How can we implement that learning in our present decisions?

17. What can we learn from the process of changes in mission for others?

   ◦ Specify your learning from the analysis of a similar process by other players in the industry.

18. What can be the process of developing the new mission?

   ◦ How should we develop or modify our mission statement?
   ◦ Should it be only the modification or the complete change of the mission statement?
   ◦ What are the reasons for it?
   ◦ How much time and effort should we dedicate to the development of the mission?
   ◦ How the operations and other workings of the organization would be affected during these changes?
   ◦ How should the mission statement be tested for its validity and rationality?
   ◦ How should we bring everything in synchronization after completing the process of mission development?

19. Who will be the people and teams involved in developing the new mission?

   ◦ What skills and competencies would be required to deliver the mission?
   ◦ How the teams would be formed, ideas discussed, and information captured and processed?

20. How can we test the relevance of the new mission?

   ◦ What would be the process of testing the relevance of the new mission statement?

- How would we know about its impact on the organization and its profitability?

21. Will our stakeholders agree with the new mission?

    - Review the comfort level of your organization's stakeholders with the new mission.

22. How will it be communicated?

    - Specify the process of communicating the new mission and its meaning to all the stakeholders of the organization.

23. How will our processes and other operations be affected by the change of mission?

    - Specify the impact of the processes and other operations of the organization would have on the redesign of the mission.

24. How will that process be managed?

    - Specify your plan to manage the process of redesigning your mission.

25. How it will change us?

    - Analyze the different ways in which the change of mission would have on the functioning of the organization.

26. Will we require any new training for our employees and workers?

    - Discuss with your human resource management team to understand the need for any new training required for its employees.

27. How will that be arranged?

    - What would that training be about and who would provide the training?

28. Will we face any resistance to the change of mission from our stakeholders?

   ◦ What type of resistance are we expecting from our different stakeholders, with the changes in the mission of the organization?

29. How will that be managed?

   ◦ What is our plan to bring the required changes to the organization?

CHAPTER TWENTY-ONE

What are our goals?

1. With the mission updated, what are our new goals?

   - How would we define our new long-term, medium-term and short-term goals based on our new mission statement?
   - How would it affect our strategy and planning?

2. What are our long-term and short-term goals?

   - Are our long-term and short-term goals in synchronization with each other?

3. What are the results we are going to achieve for each of these goals?

   - Has redefined the clear results to be achieved, resources required and efforts to be put in for achieving each of the specified goals?

4. What is the execution plan for achieving these goals?

   - What is our planning process to achieve these results?

5. How we are going to manage our risks?

   - Do we understand our risk for each of these goals?
   - What are our risk management plans?

6. How do you go about satisfying your customers and getting the most important results?

- What results do we need to get to satisfy our customers, both primary and supporting?
- Which results do we need to achieve on a priority basis?
- How can we ensure that everything works as per the plan?

7. What is our planning process?

   - Specify your planning process, to make sure that it is effective.

8. Who would be the people involved in it?

   - The planning process is an important part of organizational success as all the actions would be dependent on the planning. That's the reason we have to involve experienced, knowledgeable, and committed people in the process.

9. How would it be reviewed for effectiveness?

   - Any plan which is being prepared should be reviewed by different teams for its effectiveness. There should be a lot of discussions to remove any weaknesses from the planning

10. What would be the execution plan?

    - Based on the planning we need to define our execution plan. It would be the specific responsibility and deadlines for achieving outcomes and results.

11. Is our execution plan robust and flexible enough?

    - The execution plan must be checked for its robustness. The situation of the market is volatile and most of the events are not in the organization's control. That is the reason that is action plan should be flexible and robust simultaneously.

12. How would we track the outcomes and results?

- ○ Specify the methodology to check the outcomes and the results achieved by different teams, employees, and managers. Achievement of the required results is the only way to achieve our goals.

13. What can we learn from the planning process of other industry players?

  - ○ We should keep analyzing our competitors and other industry players for insights and ideas, which can be utilized.

14. How can we ensure constant improvement?

  - ○ An organization that is constantly growing will survive in the long run. Therefore, we must ensure constant growth and improvement for the organization. Specify your plan for question growth and improvement.

Taken together, these fundamental five questions are powerful and get right to the heart of what makes a business successful. The answers you get will provide you with the clear roadmap you need to build a highly effective -- and profitable -- venture.

Self-analysis

We have now understood the concept of fundamental questions and their meaning. We have also utilized this concept for organizations, other than non-profits. We went through the rigorous questioning rounds for each question. Now, is the time to explore its power for self-analysis and improvement.

CHAPTER TWENTY-TWO

Analysing Self

We will use the basic philosophy of the fundamental questions, and use them for understanding the self, through the set of five questions. We will then use the series of sub-questions to dig deeper into each of the fundamental questions. The objective is to get the answers to several simple, complex, and hidden questions. It would help you to understand the present and design your future.

By the end of this section of the book, we are sure about making you clearer, more confident, and better, ready to move towards success, immediately.

Questions for self-analysis

Can the fundamental questions, be applied in the life of a person? Is there any way, we can use the power of these questions, to get more clarity for our life and work, just the way the managers of the organizations get for their companies?

In this section, we have identified the ways to utilize the concept of fundamental questions, to identify the direction of our life and work. It can help us to define the areas, in which we would find maximum success and satisfaction. The answers to these questions will also make us more productive, by identifying the areas which are important to us, and the ways to focus on them.

The objective of this section is to capture the fundamental ideas of each question and to utilize the same concept to identify the sub-questions, whose answers can provide clarity and direction to the individuals.

Try to answer as many questions as possible in this section, while being completely honest and sincere while answering them. We are sure that you would discover a few unique elements about yourself and would gain strength and clarity.

The objective of self-analysis questions

- To bring clarity in your mind about yourself, your work, and your life.
- To guide your thinking towards the important areas of your life and work.
- To make you master in answering tough questions about yourself.
- To make you focus and introspect on a specific area, without any disturbance.
- To make you a solutions person rather than a problem finder.

How to use these questions

The process to use the Questions:

- It is possible that all the questions are not answered, so try to answer as many questions as you can.
- Try to be as specific as possible in your answers, which would be much more difficult, than answering in a broad or generic way.
- Be completely honest with yourself while answering these questions.
- Bring sincerity in completing the exercise, which is required to gain maximum value out of these questions.
- Once you are through with these questions, you need to create an action plan, based on the ideas generated through the answers, to bring the required changes in your life and work.
- The next step is to take action and get specific results.
- The final step is to get feedback, both from others and from yourself, to improve yourself consistently.

The five fundamental questions for self-analysis

The fundamental questions for self-analysis are:

1. What is my mission?

2. What and where I am adding value?
3. What value addition is required?
4. What results I must achieve?
5. What is the best way to achieve my mission?

Question 1- What is my mission in life

Know about your mission.

CHAPTER TWENTY-THREE

What is my mission

- Let us first understand the meaning of mission for an individual. "Mission" is "A strongly felt aim, ambition, or calling".
- It can be a specific purpose, a long-term goal, or an ambition.

Now let us dig deeper into the self-analysis question no. 1, which is, 'What is my mission?' In this section, we will cover a large number of sub-questions, which can help us to understand our purpose, mission, Long Term goals, and other concepts related to it.

The right way to do this section is to first understand the meaning of each question and answer it broadly in your mind. After each question, you should pause for some time to answer the question in your mind, without writing it down. Do it for each and every question. There could be some questions, which are not relevant to you, and can be skipped. It is up to you to identify the questions relevant to you and answer them sincerely. We can assure you that once the questioning of this section is over, you would know enough about yourself and your mission.

Once you have reached the end of the section, we suggest you come back and again start the questions from the beginning, and repeat the process. You need to understand that only thinking about the answers in the mind is not enough. most of the time it is vague, not clear. Once you write your ideas and understanding down on a piece of paper or digitally, then you have truly answered the question.

Let's move to questions.

To get more clarity about your mission, answer the following questions:

1. What do I want to achieve in life, which would make me happy, fulfilled, and satisfied, and would give me peace of mind?

   a. Specify your mission or your long-term goals or any specific ambition, which would make you happy and fulfilled.

2. How do I define success?

   a. The definition of success is different for every person. Define your own definition of success, which will give you fulfillment, satisfaction, and peace of mind.

3. When can I call myself successful?

   a. What should happen, when you would be able to call yourself successful?

   b. What you would do to get this success?

4. What is the path to reach there?

   a. Specify your direction and the plan to reach your goals, which would make you successful.

5. Who would be the stakeholders in this journey?

   a. Who would be your supporters, partners, mentors, teachers, financers, and many other people who would make you successful?

6. What challenges would be there?

   a. What obstructions and problems do you anticipate on your journey for your mission or ambition?

7. What are the risks? How can I manage them?

   a. How would I define my risk?

   b. Do I understand my risks properly? How would I be able to manage those risks?

   c. It means if the problem happens, then what would be your strategy to deal with it and keep moving forward?

8. Do I have a very strong feeling for something or have a specific ambition? Why?

   a. Specify the specific reasons for your emotional connection to a specific mission or ambition. Why is it only this is a specific goal and not anything else?

9. Is my direction good for humanity and is moral and legal?

   a. We should not be doing anything which is in any way damaging to humanity or the environment. Our aims in life should not be value damaging or troubling for anybody else.

10. Why I am calling this specific objective my mission?

    a. Specify your present objectives, which would take you toward your specific long-term goal, mission, or ambition.

11. How much time will I take to achieve my objectives?

    a. Specify the time duration you think you would be able to achieve your ambition.
    b. How have you calculated this time?
    c. Are you convinced about it?

12. How is it going to generate value?

    a. What value do I think would be generated by my mission or ambition?]

13. Define value.

    a. How would I define the value which I am going to create?

14. For whom is it going to generate value?

    a. Define the people, institutions or organizations that would get the benefits of your generated value.

CHAPTER TWENTY-FOUR

What is my purpose in life

Life's purpose

in this section, we would try to understand our purpose in life and work. Every individual should be having a specific purpose in their life and work, which would consistently motivate them and force them to take powerful actions. Most people are unable to recognize their purpose in life. If you ask anybody about their purpose in life, most people would answer "I do not know about it, maybe, to earn and live." Or they say "It is a theoretical concept. It has no meaning in practical life." Similarly, they will find a lot of reasons for not finding their purpose in life. We must have observed very motivated and committed individuals, who are leaders, living with a specific purpose in life. People are attracted to them, and these leaders can inspire those people to achieve things, which they never thought were possible. Why does that happen? It happens because we all are attracted to those people, who have clarity and direction in their lives. As many people are directionless, therefore they hope to find their purpose, with the inspiration of these leaders and mentors.

Without any purpose in life, our life becomes boring, without clarity or direction. Animals do not have any purpose in life. They live, eat, procreate, protect themselves from predators and eventually die. They only exist in their life, instead of living. Their consciousness is not evolved like humans to understand the concept of purpose, find their purpose, and dedicate their life and energy towards it.

Many politicians dedicate their life to a specific cause. Social workers have a purpose for a specific issue. Many doctors focus their life's work, on curing specific diseases. Most teachers dedicate their lives to nurturing the minds of their students, by spreading knowledge. These people are always energized and motivated in their lives because they have a specific purpose, which gives them challenges, direction, and goals.

It would be difficult to understand the power of purpose, till we have one. That is the reason we should always try to find or identify our purpose in life. We can get the answers about our mission, by answering a few questions.

The first section to understand your mission is to find your purpose.

The purpose of life

1. Why do I exist?

    a. What is the reason for my existence?
    b. Why I came to this life?
    c. What value can I add to the people, society, or community so that I transform their lives?

2. What is something, I should do or achieve so that I feel fulfilled?

    a. How can I feel fulfilled? What I would like to achieve in my life before death?

3. Does any purpose in my life exist?

    a. If you have doubts about understanding the purpose of your life, then you need to understand that every human is born with a specific purpose. They must find it. The only action they should take is to first believe in having a purpose, and then try hard to find it.

4. How can I find the purpose of my life?

    a. The purpose of life can be found by asking a few fundamental questions, as discussed before, and consistently looking for a specific cause or mission, with which you are strongly emotionally connected.

5. How I can define the purpose of my life?

    a. Define in clear words and specificity the purpose you have in your life. It can be broken down into long-term goals, which can further be broken down into medium-term and short-term goals.

6. Is my purpose practical?

    a. What is the relevance of my purpose? Is it achievable within the available time?

7. What is the relevance of this purpose?

    a. How would the actions for my purpose create value and for whom?

8. How would my life change, if I achieve my mission?

    a. How would my life enhance, when I achieve my mission? How the life of other associated people would change?

9. How would I feel, if I achieve my mission?

    a. What would be my emotional state, when I achieve my mission?

10. What would happen, if I do not achieve my mission?

    a. How would I feel if I am unable to achieve my mission, due to my lack of courage or actions?

11. Will this purpose make my life relevant for me and others?

    a. In what way, my purpose would enhance the lives of other people?
    b. Will my satisfaction level enhance after achieving my mission?

12. Is this purpose rational and achievable?

    a. Is my purpose practical?
    b. What is the relevance of my purpose?
    c. Is it achievable, within the available time?

13. Will this purpose change over time? How many years?

    a. How do I think my purpose would be impacted by time and external conditions and influences?

    b. In how many years do I think my purpose would require revision and modification?

14. What is the process of finding my purpose?

    a. What path do I need to follow for my purpose?

    b. What actions do I need to take?

    c. What type of person do I need to become for it?

15. How can I remain committed to my purpose?

    a. How can I make sure that my commitment and dedication level for my purpose, is not affected by anything or anyone?

16. How will I find energy for my purpose? How will I remain motivated?

    a. How can I maintain my motivation level for putting my efforts, energy, and resources into my purpose?

17. What can I learn from other people with similar purposes?

    a. Know about the people who have followed a similar purpose in their lives.

    b. What can I learn from them and their experiences?

18. What type of person do I need to become for my purpose?

    a. What skills do I need to develop for achieving my purpose?

    b. What changes I would need to bring in for following my purpose?

19. What abilities and competencies I must have for my purpose?

    a. What do I need to learn?

    b. How should I develop myself for achieving the goals for my purpose?

20. What support and resources I would require for my purpose?

    a. Will I require any support from anyone?
    b. What type of resources would be required for following my dreams?

21. What problems and obstructions I could face on this path? What would be the challenges?

    a. What challenges I would be facing to follow my purpose?
    b. How can I deal with these challenges, problems, and obstructions?

22. What are the risks?

    a. [What are the risks, which I could be facing, due to my decisions and actions for my purpose?

23. How can I manage these risks?

    a. Specify your risk management plan.

The next part of the process of understanding your mission is to know your goals.

CHAPTER TWENTY-FIVE

What are the major goals of my life

1. How can I define my mission/purpose in terms of long-term and short-term goals?

    a. Break down your mission or purpose in terms of LT and ST goals.
    b. Clearly define these goals by writing them down.
    c. Your short-term goals would lead to long-term goals.

2. Am I confident about achieving these goals? Will I get the feeling of fulfillment and happiness after achieving each of these goals?

    a. If you're not excited about achieving your goals, then there is some discrepancy between your goals' synchronization with your purpose.

3. What can I learn from the experience of people pursuing similar goals?

    a. What can I learn from others, about achieving these goals?

4. What is the best way to achieve my goals?

    a. What can be the best plan to achieve the identified goals?

5. How would I extract my life goals from my mission or purpose?

    a. Your specific purpose or mission in your life would have certain results and outcomes to be achieved. Those results would become your long-term goals and ambition. You can define your medium-term and short-term goals, based on these specific long-term goals.

6. What are my LT, MT, and ST goals?

    a. What are the specific results to be achieved for each of these goals?
    b. Your mission or purpose would define your long-term goals. The duration of your long-term goals would be based upon the outcomes required for your mission in life and work. They may range from 7 years to even 15 years. Every person would have their own specific duration for achieving their long-term goals. The medium-term goals would lead to the long-term goals. And, the short-term goals lead to your medium-term goals. All of these goals must be in synchronization with each other.

7. What are the deadlines to achieve these goals?

    a. You need to set optimum and relevant deadlines to achieve each of your goals. These deadlines should neither be too relaxed to make you complacent nor too stretched, making them unachievable.

8. Is there any conflict or contradiction in my goals definitions?

    a. We need to check for any contradiction or conflict in our goals. It means that the outcome of one specific goal should not resist or become an obstruction to any other goal. Our one set of goals should support other sets of goals.

9. Am I confident about achieving these goals?

    a. What is my confidence level in achieving my goals?
    b. Do I feel that my skills and competencies are enough to achieve the specified goals?
    c. What would be required to achieve my goals?
    d. How can I enhance my confidence level to achieve these goals?

10. What challenges I would be facing to pursue my goals?

a. What obstructions and challenges do I expect to face on the path to these goals?

b. Am I confident about dealing with these challenges and managing situations to achieve my goals?

11. Am I clear about the results to be achieved for these goals?

a. What is the clear definition of the outcomes to be achieved for each of my goals?

b. Am I clear about the actions to be taken to achieve the required results?

c. How can I ensure the quality of these results?

d. What is my plan to achieve the results, optimally?

The next part of the mission segment is to understand the meaning of success for you.

What is the definition of success in my life

1. How do I define success? Why?

   a. What are the main reasons for my definition of success?
   b. What has influenced me to define this definition?
   c. What are the chances for this definition of success to change in the next two years?
   d. What will happen when I would achieve success?
   e. How my definition of success would evolve over a period of time?

2. Is this definition of success rational, achievable, moral, and sustainable?

   a. Everybody has a different definition of success for themselves in their personal and professional life.
   b. Define what success means to you.
   c. 'Why' of your life, is important to answer because it would give you the required motivation for moving forward.

3. What value would be created with my success? For whom the value is being generated?

   a. Define the value generated by your success.
   b. Describe the people, entities, institutions, or organizations, that would be benefitted from the value generated by your success.
   c. Is there any way to enhance the value generated from your success?

4. Is it damaging value for anyone in any way?

    a. Is there any negative aspect to my success?
    b. How can I make sure that the negative aspect is either eliminated or managed properly?
    c. Who would be affected by the negative aspect of my success?

5. Why do I have a strong emotional connection with the present definition of success?

    a. Why anything else is not a success for me?

Question 2- What and where am I adding value?

Do you know what and how are you creating value for self and others?

CHAPTER TWENTY-SEVEN

What and where am I adding value?

Now let us dig deeper into the self-analysis question no. 2, which is, 'What and where am I adding value?' In this section, we will cover a large number of sub-questions, which can help us to understand our value addition and other concepts related to it.

The right way to do this section is to first understand the meaning of each question and answer it broadly in your mind. After each question, you should pause for some time to answer the question in your mind, without writing it down. Do it for each and every question. There could be some questions, which are not relevant to you, and can be skipped. It is up to you to identify the questions relevant to you and answer them sincerely. We can assure you that once the questioning of this section is over, you would know enough about yourself and the value you are adding.

Once you have reached the end of the section, we suggest you come back and again start the questions from the beginning, and repeat the process. You need to understand that only thinking about the answers in the mind is not enough. most of the time it is vague, not clear. Once you write your ideas and understanding down on a piece of paper or digitally, then you have truly answered the question.

Let's move to questions.

1. What are my responsibilities to achieve my mission?

    a. What responsibilities and initiation do I need to take to achieve my mission?
    b. What would be the challenges?
    c. How can I make sure to deal with these challenges?

2. Who are the people, organizations, entities, and institutions I love and want to serve?

   a. Define the people, individuals, communities, and organizations, whom you want to serve and they mean a lot to you. It can be a self, family, country, community, special cause, objective, or goal.

3. Why should I be serving only specified entities, not anybody else? Why my focus must be clear?

   a. You need to know the reasons for your focus on a specific goal and mission. You need to know your 'why'. Without knowing your 'why', it would be difficult for you to get motivated.

4. What is my definition of value?

   a. Define the value which you are generating and for whom.

5. Why can I call the people I serve as my customers?

   a. For a person, a customer would be the people, individuals, communities, or organizations which are getting the benefit out of the value generated by that person. For example, for a social worker, the customers would be the community of people, for whom she is working.]

6. What will happen if I do not serve them or give them value?

   a. It is assumed that the value generated by an individual's work enhances the life of other people she is serving. For example, people work for themselves and their families. It means that a person's family would get the benefit of the value generated by that person. We need to know about the changes, which would come if we do not generate the required value.

7. Who are not my customers?

a. We also need to get clarity about the people, whom we are not serving. The more our value is focused, the better and more impactful it would be. We need to clearly define the focus of our generated value. We also need to know about any wastage or leakage in our generated value.

8. What are the forces which can damage the value? What can be my role to deal with these opposing forces?

9. Is the definition of my value and the value of my customers in synchronization?

a. What can be the discrepancy in understanding the value for my customers?
b. Is my definition of value similar to other people, who are also dealing with similar situations and customers?
c. What are the reasons for these differences, if any?
d. How can I deal with these differences?

10. Is anything immoral or illegal associated with my actions? If yes, then what changes are required in my thinking and actions?

a. Everything which I do needs to be moral and legal, otherwise, it would be damaging for everyone involved.

11. in what way serving my customers, would give me value?

a. When we serve somebody, we expect a certain value in return. For example, a teacher would expect love and affection from her students.
b. What value do I expect from the people and entities, I am serving?

12. Are my actions rational and logical? Am I completely satisfied with my actions?

a. Analyze your actions and independently evaluate their rationality and potential for value generation. You need to check your satisfaction level with your actions and expected results. If you do not find your actions to be rational or satisfactory, then you need to review your actions again, for required changes.

13. In what way my life will change, if I start to serve my customers in the best possible way? Your objective should be to satisfy your customers and do everything, that is expected from you.

   a. What is my understanding of the results I am getting and the value I am generating?
   b. Is there any way to generate more value out of your present actions and endeavors?
   c. What would happen if you start working at your peak performance level?

14. What will happen if I am unable to satisfy my customers?

   a. Define the possible happenings if you are unable to generate the required value as expected from you.
   b. How can we make sure that never happens?

15. What can you learn from the experience of other people, who have the same set of customers or who are serving the same set of customers?

   a. Who are the people generating similar value, for the same type of people and entities?
   b. What is my observation and understanding of these people?
   c. What can we learn from these people?

16. How can I make sure that I do not do anything wrong – which is immoral or illegal?

   a. What can be illegal or immoral in my actions?
   b. How can I make sure that never happens?

17. Should I change the definition of my customers frequently?

   a. What would be the conditions in which the definitions of my customers would change?
   b. What these changes would be?

c. What do I need to be careful about?

d. The definition of customers can change slightly based on time, environment, and conditions. You need to be clear about the definition of your customers or the people and organizations you are serving, in addition to the results to be achieve

18. How can I add value to the people and organizations associated with me so that I become indispensable, and receive love, respect, affection, and get success?

Question 3- What value addition is required?

Do you know what is required from you?

What value addition is required?

Now let us dig deeper into the self-analysis question no. 3, which is, 'What value addition is required?' In this section, we will cover a large number of sub-questions, which can help us to understand the value addition required in our life and work and other concepts related to it.

The right way to do this section is to first understand the meaning of each question and answer it broadly in your mind. After each question, you should pause for some time and answer the question in your mind, without writing it down. Do it for each and every question. There could be some questions, which are not relevant to you, and can be skipped. It is up to you to identify the questions relevant to you and answer them sincerely. We can assure you that once the questioning of this section is over, you would know enough about yourself and the value you should be adding.

Once you have reached the end of the section, we suggest you come back and again start the questions from the beginning, and repeat the process. You need to understand that only thinking about the answers in the mind is not enough. most of the time it is vague, not clear. Once you write your ideas and understanding down on a piece of paper or digitally, then you have truly answered the question.

Let's move to questions.

1. What is the higher and lower limit of value generation for the customers?

    a. Define the value to be generated and specify the minimum value to be generated and the maximum value which you can generate.

2. What resources I would be required, and what support I would be needing to generate this value?

    a. Identify the resources and support you would be required for generating the required value.

3. What are the risks to generate this value?

    a. What is the analysis of your risk to generate the required value?

4. How can we manage these risks?

    a. Specify your strategy to manage each of these risks, so that either they are eradicated or their impact is drastically reduced.

5. Is there anything I am missing or not considering?

    a. Recheck your understanding of the value and the whole plan of generating value. Look for any gaps, weaknesses, or problems.

6. What are the right and most productive ways of generating value?

    a. Look from a fresh mind for ways to generate the required value in a better and more efficient way.

7. Is my process of value generation damaging value for anybody or in any way?

    a. This is an important point to check that the value you are generating should not destroy value for anybody else in any way. If that is happening then our value generation plan will not be sustainable.

8. Who are the stakeholders in this value-generation process?

    a. Identify all the associated people in the value-generation process.

Question 4- What results I must achieve?

The results to achieve to feel satisfied and fulfilled.

What results I must achieve?

Now let us dig deeper into the self-analysis question no. 3, which is, 'What results I must achieve?' In this section, we will cover a large number of sub-questions, which can help us to understand the results and outcomes we need to achieve and other concepts related to it.

The right way to do this section is to first understand the meaning of each question and answer it broadly in your mind. After each question, you should pause for some time and answer the question in your mind, without writing it down. Do it for each and every question. There could be some questions, which are not relevant to you, and can be skipped. It is up to you to identify the questions relevant to you and answer them sincerely. We can assure you that once the questioning of this section is over, you would know enough about your organization and its customers.

Once you have reached the end of the section, we suggest you come back and again start the questions from the beginning, and repeat the process. You need to understand that only thinking about the answers in the mind is not enough. most of the time it is vague, not clear. Once you write your ideas and understanding down on a piece of paper or digitally, then you have truly answered the question.

Let's move to questions.

1. What are the results I want to achieve?

    a. Specify in clear terms the results, which you want to achieve both in the long-term and short term. The objective of the results is to achieve your goals and to get the feeling of fulfillment (this feeling gives you satisfaction and happiness). Every goal successfully achieved, would move you closer to your ambition and mission.

2. Why do I think that the specified results are the right results?

   a. What makes me sure that the specified results are the results, which should be achieved?
   b. Is it possible that I don't want to achieve any results, it could be the journey for a specific purpose, which I need to enjoy.

3. What would be required to put my full force into it?

   a. What is the reason which would motivate you to put your energy and full force towards achieving these results?
   b. How can we sustain this superior performance level?

4. What I will do and what I will not do to get results?

   a. Specify the rules, which you would be following to get the results. Principles that would form the backbone of your actions and the activities which you would never do. For example, in your journey towards your goals, you decide to never break anybody's trust or cheat someone for your benefit.

5. How will I sustain success?

   a. Putting in initial efforts is easy while sustaining success is always difficult. Specify the ways to ensure that you would be able to sustain your efforts and your success.

6. What are the results, which I need to achieve?

   a. There is a difference between want and need. Are your "results what you want" and "results what you need" are same? If not, on which results would you focus?

7. Why do I want only these outcomes, why not something else?

   a. Specify the reasons for focusing on these outcomes and results.

8. What is the direction I need to take to achieve these outcomes?

a. If you know about your goals and results to be achieved, you must be sure about the direction you should be taking. You need to move toward your bigger goals, ambition, mission, and purpose. Everything must be in synchronization.

9. Why only this direction I must take, why not anything else?

a. This is a question to check your understanding of the direction you have planned or are presently taking. It is questioning your fundamental mission and purpose. Do you want to recheck it?

10. What would happen if I take a different direction or a different approach for achieving the same results?

a. It is a question about rechecking your planning. What could be the different ways of achieving your outcomes?
b. What could be the best way to achieve results?

11. Is the definition of these results clear to me?

a. You need to understand the meaning of the results, which you aim to achieve.

12. What could be the reasons for the change of perceptions for these results?

a. How do you perceive these results?
b. What can be the different perceptions of these results?
c. Is there any way that my perception of these results would change?

13. What is the time limit for achieving these results – both optimistic and pessimistic? What approach do I need to take?

a. What are my expectations about the time duration of achieving these results? What is my prediction in both the optimistic (how soon I will be able to achieve results) and the pessimistic way (if everything goes wrong then how much time will it take)?

14. What would be my next set of results, if I achieve these results?

    a. Do I have any idea about my next set of goals, after I achieve my present goals?

15. What would happen if I am unable to achieve these results?

    a. What actions do I need to take, if I am unable to achieve my results?

16. Are these results moral and legal in every way? If not, what do I need to do?

    a. Are the results I am going to achieve, right in every sense (that is, they are rational, achievable, moral, and legal)

17. How would I take the feedback?

    a. Specify the ways you would take feedback on your actions and performance.

18. Who would provide the feedback to me?

    a. The feedback provided needs, to be honest, and straightforward, to get the true benefit out of it. Who would be the people providing feedback to me?

19. How would I analyze the feedback?

    a. Specify the processes you would use to analyze the feedback received.

20. How would my actions be changed or modified based on feedback?

    a. Specify the ways you would utilize the analysis of feedback to enhance your actions for results.

21. How often should I be taking the feedback?

a. Specify the timing and duration when you should be taking the feedback.

22. How much should I rely on these feedbacks?

   a. All the feedbacks are not beneficial or correct. They are just to give us an understanding of the opinion or perception of a specific person. We need to utilize these feedbacks with rationality. We need to have the understanding of taking the real value out of the feedback received from others.

23. What are the important points I need to keep in mind while taking these feedbacks?

   a. Specify the rules you would be following for getting these feedbacks.

24. What should happen to make my journey interesting, for achieving results?

   a. How can you ensure that you enjoy the journey toward your goals?

25. What is the best way of achieving results?

   a. Review the path you are following for achieving the results.
   b. Can there be a better way?

26. In which areas can I go wrong, while pursuing results?

   a. Based on your understanding of yourself and the analysis of the actions to be taken, think about the areas which could be complex for you.

27. How often should I be reviewing my results to be achieved?

   a. You need to keep reviewing the results, you have to achieve. It helps you to keep the actions at the top of your mind and guides you towards better actions.

28. What are the chances that the results would be changed?

    a. There is a possibility that the results, which we are trying to achieve are changed in some way. We need to look for that possibility.

29. How these results are linked to my mission and my customers?

    a. How the results which I am trying to achieve would help me to generate value for the people, entities, and organization I love and care, about and help me to move towards my mission.

30. Are these results my path to satisfaction and peace of mind?

    a. Will the goals I'm trying to achieve lead me to satisfaction and peace of mind, which is the final objective for most people?

31. Are these results part of my definition of success?

    a. Analyze the synchronization of your results to be achieved and your understanding of success.]

32. What is the view of other people about these results?

    a. What is the opinion of other people about my goals and the results I am trying to achieve?
    b. Why do they have those views?

33. Am I utilizing my talent, energy, and my potential for achieving these results or are they getting wasted in some way?

    a. A person gets satisfaction only when he is able to utilize his potential and skills while growing in the process.
    b. Are you growing in the process of achieving your goals or not?

34. Are these results driving true value for me and others?
35. Recheck the value generated by your actions and its impact on you and others.

36. What is my learning from my experience? What is my learning from others' experiences?

   a. What I have learned till now?
   b. What do I expect to learn in the future?

Question 5- What is the best way to achieve my mission?

The Right path.

CHAPTER THIRTY

What is the best way to achieve my mission?

Now let us dig deeper into the fundamental question no. 5, which is, 'What is the best way to achieve my mission?' In this section, we will cover a large number of sub-questions, which can help us to understand our plan and strategy to achieve the required goals, outcomes, and results.

The right way to do this section is to first understand the meaning of each question and answer it broadly in your mind. After each question, you should pause for some time and answer the question in your mind, without writing it down. Do it for each and every question. There could be some questions, which are not relevant to you, and can be skipped. It is up to you to identify the questions relevant to you and answer them sincerely. We can assure you that once the questioning of this section is over, you would know enough about yourself, and the actions you need to take.

Once you have reached the end of the section, we suggest you come back and again start the questions from the beginning, and repeat the process. You need to understand that only thinking about the answers in the mind is not enough. most of the time it is vague, not clear. Once you write your ideas and understanding down on a piece of paper or digitally, then you have truly answered the question.

Let's move to questions.

The best way to achieve my mission, purpose, and goals.

1. What is the best way of achieving the goals, which I have set for myself? Both long-term and short-term?

    a. Understand your goals, defining them clearly by writing them down. Your ambition, mission, purpose, and long-term goals would define your medium-term and short-term goals and the results to be achieved.

2. What person do I need to become to achieve these goals?

   a. For achieving these goals, you have to transform yourself uniquely, so that you are equipped with the skills to achieve your goals.

3. Is it difficult or easy?

   a. How do you rate the process of achieving your goals in terms of complexity?
   b. How are you going to make yourself confident enough to put your full force into achieving these goals?

4. How is it going to change my life?

   a. Specify how your life and the life of your loved ones would change after achieving these goals. Can you strongly feel those changes emotionally?

5. What changes I would need to bring in my life and actions to become that person, who would get results?

   a. Specify the changes which you need to bring in your behavior, thinking, decision-making, and actions to transform yourself into a person to achieve your goals.

6. What challenges I would need to face?

   a. Identify the challenges, which you need to face to change yourself as a person.

7. What hindrances and obstructions could block me?

   a. Identify the expected hindrances, obstructions, and problems, which you may face to pursue your goals.

8. How do I plan to serve?

    a. In what way you would be delivering the value to the people for whom it is being generated?

9. What actions and decisions do I need to take?

    a. Specify the immediate decisions and actions you would take.

10. What can I learn from others' experiences in achieving their goals and delivering value?

    a. Study other people who have either achieved their goals or are struggling to achieve their goals.
    b. What can we learn from these people?

11. What are my risks?

    a. Specify your risks on the path to achieving your goals.

12. What is my plan for risk management?

    a. Think about your risk management plan for each of the specified risks.

13. Am I satisfied with this plan? Is there anything, which I find missing, or is with a gap?

    a. What is your confidence level with the plan?
    b. Is anything missing?
    c. If you're not feeling comfortable with your plan, then it is better either to improve it or rework it from scratch.

14. What is required to be done, for generating the required value to achieve my mission?

    a. What would be my initial achievements, to generate the required value?

15. What actions do I need to take?

    a. Write a list of actions, which you need to take and the results to be achieved in the next three months.

16. Which are the hard decisions, which are required to be taken?

    a. Identify the most complex decisions, which you need to take.
    b. Why are you calling them complex?
    c. How can you take these decisions in the best possible way?

17. How fast can I take these decisions?

    a. What is our plan to make sure that you do not waste a lot of time on these decisions?

18. How can I make sure that my execution is perfect and effective?

    a. Execution is the most important part of achieving results. You need to be completely confident about your plan and your competencies.
    b. How can you ensure your high confidence level for the execution stage?

19. How can I make sure that my high level of productivity is maintained?

    a. How can I make sure that I remain productive during my actions?

20. Do I need to plan for it?

    a. You must deal with your self-doubts.

21. What is the direction I need to take?

    a. Recheck the direction you are taking for achieving your goals

22. What is the strategy I need to follow?

    a. Recheck the strategy you are following for achieving the desired results.

23. What I must do and what I should not be doing?

    a. What are the basic rules, which I would be following on the path toward goals?

24. What type of support I would need?

    a. Ensure the support which you would be requiring. The lack of resources should not be affecting your productivity and your motivation for achieving results.

25. What type of resources I would require? [Recheck the required resources, skills, and competencies to achieve results.

26. What can go wrong? How can I manage it?

    a. What is my understanding of the problems, obstructions, and hindrances, which I would be facing to achieve results?
    b. What is my plan to deal with them?
    c. Am I confident about it?

27. What can I learn from the execution and planning of other people, who are successful in similar activities?

    a. Specify your learning after studying other people, so that you do not make their mistakes.

28. How everything will change, if the definition of value, my customers, and my mission changes?

    a. Think about the alternative reality if the definition of value, your present customers, and your future goals change completely.
    b. How will I make sure that I can deal with those drastic changes?
    c. Why that change would occur?

29. What would be the stimulus and the conditions, which would bring that change?

    a. Think about the events, situations, and conditions, which would lead to these drastic changes. Don't worry, this is a rare possibility. It is only a thought experiment, allowing you to expand your thinking abilities.

30. What type of changes would be required in my thinking and my actions?

    a. Think about the different changes, which would be required in your thinking process, decision-making, and actions.

31. What can go wrong?

    a. Identify the areas where problems can pop up with your mistakes and blunders.

32. How can I manage it?

    a. Specify the mindset and strategies, if any, to deal with these mistakes and blunders.

The last five questions

Based on your previous self-analysis, answer the last five questions.

1. Where I am now?
2. Where do I have to reach?
3. What is the gap? [define the gap between your present position and your ambition or mission.]
4. What do I need to do to fill this gap?
5. What is my action plan?

End

Now you have the model and tools to transform your organization and life. Use the fundamental questions as your basis to analyze and look for solutions.

Take powerful action by putting your full force into the plan and sustain it, till you reach your goals.